Wheels of Injustice

Saving My Child
from the Child Savers

Second Edition

Susan Louise Gabriel

Second Edition

Wheels of Injustice: Saving My Child from the Child Savers
by Susan Louise Gabriel

ISBN-13: 9781735537054
© Susan Louise Gabriel
Independently Published

Soul SONshine™

Dedicated to my best friend
and constant companion, Jesus

Table of Contents

Preface v

1. The Alien Encounter 1

2. Stolen Identity 5

3. Where Do I Go to Get a Personality? 10

4. Desperate to Stop Dropping My Fruit Cocktail 14

5. A Scoop of Depression with a Cherry on Top 20

6. Then There Were Two 24

7. The Not-So-Chosen People 28

8. Technically Speaking 32

9. The Man Who Believed in Me 36

10. The End of Life as I Knew It 40

11. Cartwheels Down the Stairs 43

12. Starting Over Newly Hatched 47

13. Day One of the Best of My Life 50

14. How I Stopped Being Someone Else 54

15. Perfect is a Lonely Peak 59

16. Living Life in Living Color 64

17. A Norman Rockwell Thanksgiving 67

18. Bunny Hopping on the Bunny Slope 71

19. He Married Me for My Ankles 75

20. Curly, Dimpled Lunatics 79

21. Space Shuttles and Spaceships 85

22. Dropped on Another Planet 89

23. Examined by Aliens 93

24. Questions with No Answers 97

25. The Professional Child Abusers.................................102

26. And Then I Died—or So I Thought..........................106

27. The Rest of the Story 110

28. The Wheels Grind...114

29. All Rise..118

30. The Verdict is In 122

31. Picking Up the Pieces 126

32. All's Fair in War..131

33. Raising Our Voices 135

34. Higher and Higher...139

35. The New V.O.C.A.L. Majority..............................144

36. Shouting Down the Walls of Jericho 150

37. Making a Federal Case Out of It...........................156

38. Wash, Rinse, Repeat...161

39. Personality Pinball 165

40. Evil Twin...168

Derailing the Wheels of Injustice 173

Epilogue..177

Endnotes...183

Acknowledgement

◻◇●◇◻

This book would not have been written without the prodding, encouragement, and suggestions given to me by two extraordinary online friends, Drew and Isaiah. No last names are needed. You know who you are.

Preface

◻◇●◇◻

W E KNEW WITHIN the hour that he was gone.

Our Chihuahua puppy Andy didn't come in from the backyard with the other dogs. We searched every foot of the small backyard, and then we saw it—a small strip where the fence didn't quite reach all the way to the ground. The gap was just high enough for a rat or small rabbit—or Andy—to slip under.

We went door-to-door. We called his name. We looked under every bush. No Andy.

By the time it got dark, I was frantic, but we had to stop looking because it was too dark to see anything clearly, even with a flashlight.

I made flyers that night and printed a hundred of them. Early the next morning, I went door-to-door, handing them out or attaching them to residents' door handles.

I just prayed that someone had found him. The outside temperature had been around 50 degrees the night before, which is really cold for a Chihuahua with little to no hair.

I took the day off from work and passed out flyers all day, going to every house within a two-mile radius. As I walked, I eyed the hawks circling overhead and tried not to think about how much Andy looked like a gray rat.

That night around 9 p.m. my melancholy mood was interrupted by a phone call. It was a neighbor who lived about two miles away. He'd seen our flyer, and he'd just seen Andy!

Andy was at a pond near the man's house. The man tried calling to him, but Andy was frightened and ran away.

My husband Clark and I jumped into our SUV and drove to the place where Andy had been spotted, but he wasn't there.

With the windows unrolled, we slowly drove down each street that surrounded the pond, calling loudly for him.

Then Clark said, "Look behind us!" I turned around, and there was Andy, trotting behind the SUV as fast as his little legs would carry him, trying to catch up to us.

We had a joyful reunion. Andy celebrated with a chicken dinner, which he gobbled down like a ravenous wolf. And he's been a faithful follower ever since.

Now I live in a house that sits on an acre of land in the country. When I go for a walk, three of our four dogs wander around the property, letting every new scent carry them to the next clump of grass. But Andy never wanders. He watches my feet and follows me—four feet behind—until I eventually return to the house.

I want to follow Jesus the same way Andy follows me—with complete trust—knowing that no matter the destination, it's all good.

As I learned from Andy—just focus on the feet.

◻◇●◇◻

The Treasure Map

Watch my feet. Your trust will grow
and you will know which way to go.
Don't try to find the road alone.
Don't try to do it on your own.
Just pray and follow, I advise.
I'll take you where your treasure lies.

◻◇●◇◻

*Store up for yourselves **treasures in heaven**, where moths and vermin do not destroy, and where thieves do not break in and steal. For where your treasure is, there your heart will be also.* —Mathew 6: 20-21, NIV

◻◇●◇◻

The events in this book vividly live on in my memory. I've recorded them here to send you courage in your own struggles and peace from fear.

Dietrich Bonhoeffer was an inspiring Christian pastor who dared to oppose Hitler and tried to stop the Nazi movement. He died a martyr's death but left behind a legacy and this quote, which captures and parallels the essence of what this book is about.

> We are not to simply bandage the wounds of victims beneath the wheels of injustice, we are to drive a spoke into the wheel itself.

Similarly—but on a different level—I fought to "drive a spoke into the wheel" of a powerful system that recklessly mangled families beneath its wheels. My battle with the system is over, but my battle to live a victorious Christian life, following Jesus as my leader, is ongoing.

I know you have battles of your own. I hope you find inspiration in these pages to take up your own sword and shield and fearlessly step into battle.

This war is NOT over.

An Introductory Note

▫◇●◇▫

This story focuses on events in my life that contributed toward making me the person I am today. I wrote about them from the perspective of how I viewed the events and how I felt about them at the time. I have grown since then. I hope that becomes apparent in later chapters.

I am not proud of some of the attitudes and behaviors I exhibited. However, I include them to give an honest account of my life because I want readers to see how God loved me—a weak and damaged individual with sometimes a poor attitude—and used me for His glory. And in doing so, He gave me joy, hope, and gratitude for His gracious love and forgiveness.

May you experience the same joy, hope, and gratitude in your own life.

-1-

The Alien Encounter

□◇●◇□

W EDNESDAY, FEBRUARY 12, 1986, dawns bright but cold. I kiss nine-year-old Emily goodbye and watch her walk across the courtyard to the babysitter's apartment. She will walk to school—a block away—with the babysitter's daughter, who is two years older than Emily.

My older daughter, 15-year-old Amber, is temporarily living with her Aunt Wanda so she's not available to walk Emily to school today.

Then I leave for work. And while I'm not looking, an alien spaceship sets its course for earth.

"Sue, phone call," a voice calls out.

It's just after lunch. I walk to the desk in the test area where the push-button style phone sits.

"Mrs. Clark?" says a voice I don't recognize.

"No, this is Mrs. Gabriel. Clark is my husband's first name."

"This is Paula Randall of the Child Welfare Division of the Department of Social Services—DSS. We wanted you to know that we have your daughter."

"You what? You have Amber? Why isn't she in school?" My mind starts racing, trying to piece together what she is saying. "Is she hurt?"

1

"No, Ms. Clark, er... Gabrielle..."

"It's Gabriel." I interrupt her.

Who is this lady? I think. *She can't even get my name right! Is this some kind of scam?*

"Let me talk to Amber," I demand.

"She's not here. It's not about her," she responds in an increasingly tense voice. "We have your other daughter, Emily."

The bottom drops out of my stomach and hits the floor as my brain starts bouncing against the far wall, trying to make sense of her words.

My teen Amber—she's the one who's been causing me grief lately. But she said **"Emily."**

"You have Emily? Emily?? WHY?!"

"We need you to come down to the DSS facility and we will talk about that."

I barely stay on the phone long enough to get directions. Then I race back to my test station to grab my coat and purse. I briefly tell Jim I have an emergency with Emily and must leave as I hurry down the hall and out to the car.

I don't remember the drive, but I'm sure I broke speed limits. The next thing I remember is being seated in an uncomfortable chair in a small, cold, and sterile room across from a small, cold, and sterile-looking woman.

"Where is Emily?" I ask for at least the third time.

"We will get to that in a minute," she responds. "First, I want to ask about Clark. Who is he? Your boyfriend?"

"Clark is my husband, but what does that..."

Miss cold-and-sterile interrupts and says that Emily is being held in another room. "Held in another room?"

She makes it sound like she's a criminal—what did she do?

She then tells me the one thing I didn't see coming, the very last thing I expected because the thought of it had not and would never have entered my head.

I don't see it yet, but the alien spaceship just entered the earth's atmosphere.

Over the next few minutes, she tells me Emily has revealed that she was sexually molested by Clark.

And just like that, the aliens smash into our little family.

To say I am shocked is an understatement. To say I am shocked speechless, that all the blood drains from my head, that I feel faint and sick and hot and cold, and highly, highly confused, all at the same time, is still an understatement.

"Can I talk to Emily?" I ask when I am finally able to speak again. "I'm sure it's a misunderstanding. If I could just talk..."

Miss cold-and-sterile interrupts again. "No. It's better in these cases if we sort through it first."

Sort through what?

I search my memory. Had Clark really done something like that? It doesn't ring true. Clark doesn't seem like that type. We have a great—and frequent—physical relationship. We've only been married six weeks, and we are still on our "honeymoon."

"What did Emily say happened?" I finally ask.

"She said that Clark tickled her."

Did I hear her right? Did she say that Clark tickled her? Is that a crime now?

"Where?" I ask.

She points to her stomach region. "Here. Around the belly button. And her chest."

Wait, what?

A memory of Clark tickling a giggling Emily on the stomach appears in my mind.

Then a vision of Emily holding onto Clark like a drowning victim and Clark tickling her armpits to get her to finally let go pops into my head.

Does this lady consider a flat-chested nine-year-old's armpits the "chest?"

3

I search my memory for anything more sinister. And I can't remember anything that could even remotely be called sexual molestation.

"Clark is living in your home, correct?" When I nod, she continues, "We will keep Emily for a little while to give you enough time to tell Clark he has to move out. You must demonstrate your full support of Emily, or you may not get your daughter back."

"What are you talking about?" I almost shout. "I just got married!"

"In that case, it should be pretty simple. I strongly advise a divorce since you got married such a short time ago. Once that's accomplished, we will talk about letting Emily return to your home under our supervision."

What on earth...wait—is this still earth?? What is she saying?

My mouth goes dry, and I feel faint again.

"Where will Emily be?" I finally ask when I have enough saliva to speak.

"We will hold her in foster care until we have finished our investigation and feel that it's safe for her to return home. But she can't return as long as Clark is living in your home. And I advise you not to get an attorney—that will just make you look guilty."

*What is **wrong** with this woman?*

"It's safe for her to return now. What you describe is NOT sexual molestation! Can I talk with your supervisor?" I ask.

Miss cold-and-sterile stands up, walks to the door of the small room, and holds it open as if inviting me to leave. Without Emily.

"You will need to make an appointment for that. She's off-site right now," she says as she walks me to the front desk to sign out.

I drive home dazed and concussed, having just been squarely hit by an alien spaceship I never even knew existed.

-2-

Stolen Identity

□◇●◇□

WHEN I WAS FOUR, I was so eager to learn to read that my mother talked the school district into allowing me to start school early. It was in kindergarten where I ran headlong into my first conundrum: What's your name?

It turns out the name I grew up answering to—the name I believed all my life was mine—was, in fact, not really my name.

My name is—wait—WHAT? WILMA?? Well, THAT'S a stupid name! And sounds nothing like Susie!

Mrs. Oughtred, the kindergarten teacher, peers at me over the paper, "Hello there, Wilma!"

I stare at her blankly, then look at my mom, who says, "Yes, Wilma is on her birth certificate, but we call her "Susie.""

Mrs. Oughtred replies, "Well, I will call her Wilma because we already have a Susan in the class, and that can be so confusing!"

I look at my mother again, hoping for—I don't know what, but she doesn't say anything.

At home, my mother explains to me that Wilma is the name on my birth certificate, while Susie is my nickname, given to me by Aunt Mamie when I was just a few months old.

I later found out that Aunt Mamie often called me "Sister Susie," and my brother, only two years old at the time, thought that was my real name, so it stuck. Always curious, I found out that "Sister Susie" came from a popular 1914 song called "Sister Susie's Sewing Shirts for Soldiers."[1] Try saying THAT three times fast.

I spent the next few months trying to get used to some other girl using my name and the teacher calling me Wilma. And Mrs. Oughtred became the first person in my life who, in an effort to create order, instead created chaos.

My teachers called me Wilma. My family called me Susie.

By second grade, I still didn't like being called Wilma. She was a comma, an unremarkable and boring form of punctuation. Wilma sat quietly at her desk and got good grades.

Susie was an exclamation mark, a silver-white horse with a flowing mane, jumping fences and running like the wind. Or a circus performer, climbing the tether ball pole like a monkey, all the way to the top, while crowds cheered her amazing and dangerous feat.

Just before school was out for the summer, the C's on the blackboard started looking like O's, and the teacher sent a note home to my parents recommending an eye doctor.

The eyeglasses my parents bought me turned the O's back into C's, but every few months, my vision grew worse, and each new pair of glasses had thicker lenses. The lenses distorted all but a small center portion of my viewing area.

Susie, the horse with the flowing mane, was put out to pasture because jumping fences required depth perception she no longer had. Wilma, the gawky girl with thick glasses got good grades, but didn't have many friends.

When I was nine years old, my mom left me at the hospital to get my tonsils removed. I was scared, and they lied to me. They said I would get to eat ice cream, but they didn't bring me any ice cream. In fact, they didn't give me anything to eat or drink at all. And they didn't tell me that my mother was going to leave me alone all night.

They took away my glasses so I couldn't see anything except white ghosts.

◻◇●◇◻

I hardly sleep, and hours later they come in and put me on a cot with wheels. They take me into a strange-smelling room with people who wear masks.

They put something over my nose and mouth.[2]

What are they doing?! I'm going to suffocate!!

I try to get away, but they're too strong, and the air is filled with a terrible medicine smell. I try to hold my breath. Someone says, "Take a breath, take a breath."

The voice gets louder. A terrible monotone. My head pounds and I think it will explode.

A ball of light pulses like the sun in the center of a tightly clenched fist. The monotone voice drones louder and louder—not shouting—more like steadily increasing the volume on a radio. The light shines brighter and brighter.

The light hurts my eyes, the fist clenches tighter and tighter, like the pounding in my head, and the voice gets louder and louder—take a breath, take a breath, TAKE A BREATH!

Then, suddenly, it stops.

I am floating above a place where millions of people are standing, but I am not one of them. I have been brought here to watch.

"Take a breath" is no longer just a bunch of words. It is here and alive. It feels like something bad disguised as something good.

"Take a breath," it says to the people in a coaxing voice. "Take a breath, take a breath, take a breath." I am so scared, I want to cry and run away, but I can't. I am suspended in air.

Some of the people listen and follow the voice. Others resist. Some people take a long time to decide what to do. I wonder what it means to take a breath.

7

As I watch, the people eventually move apart to become two separate groups. My heart pounds and I am in suspense, waiting to see what happens.

I also wonder what will happen to me. Did I take a breath?

The drama ends, and the people who had listened to the voice and took a breath are obscured in darkness. Those who resisted the voice are surrounded by light, but it's a happy light. The light is so bright, I can see right through them.

I feel happiness radiating from them and flowing toward me like a hot campfire.

I want to be happy like that. I want to go with them.

I become aware of a terrible pain that starts in the back of my throat and goes down into my chest.

My mother's voice says, "I think she's waking up."

For years, my young mind, too inexperienced and undeveloped to fully comprehend analogies or metaphors, brooded over that dream, turning it around like a Rubik's cube, trying to decipher its meaning. The passing years eventually eroded the original terror of the ether-induced dream, and for quite a while, I just thought it was silly.

I now believe that God was working through the dream to instill in me a drive to identify deceit and resist persuasion, to listen whenever my heart tells me, here is evil, disguised as good. Now whenever I recall that dream, I also remember the verses from John Chapter 10:

> *"My sheep hear My voice and I know them, and they follow Me.... they will by no means follow a stranger, but will flee from him, for they do not know the voice of strangers." -* John 10:27 & John 10:5, NKJV

□◇●◇□

The same year I had the tonsillectomy, I dreamed I died, and when I awoke, I thought I was dead. I got ready for school, walked to school, and sat in class all day thinking I was dead and no one else knew it.

I went home, went to sleep, got up the next morning, and thought I must still be dead. I wasn't sure what happened to people after they died, so the idea that they just continued leading the life they had lived while alive didn't seem all that hard for me to believe.

Day after day, I became more and more sad to be dead. I didn't talk to anyone, and everyone mostly ignored me. I didn't want to be dead. I wanted to be alive and have people know I was there. I wanted the other kids to talk to me again and invite me to play games at recess. Every day was sadder than the day before.

About two weeks later, I decided to tell Mom about the dream and ask her if I was dead. She searched my face to see if I was serious. When she saw that I was, she reassured me that I most definitely was alive, and that people went to heaven after they died.

After that, I often thought about what heaven must be like and sometimes wondered if other people were real. Were they real like me, or did they only live in my imagination? Was there any way to know for sure?

Dear God, please make me normal. I don't want to be weird. I want to be like everybody else.

-3-

Where Do I Go to Get a Personality?

◻◇●◇◻

WHEN I WAS TEN, I had a crush on a boy who liked another girl. I finally mustered up the courage to ask him why he didn't like me, and he said, "Because you don't have any personality."

Wow, that really stung. For years, I pondered how I could get a personality, why I didn't have a personality, and what exactly WAS a personality, anyway? It was truly a riddle. I analyzed his words. He didn't say I had a BAD personality, he said I didn't have ANY personality.

How was that possible?

I analyzed the girl he did like. She was cute and funny, but also, even at ten, precociously flirtatious, although I hadn't known how to describe it back then. His remark influenced my self-image for years.

With a few exceptions, I had trouble making and keeping friends throughout most of my grade school years. I just couldn't seem to figure out where NORMAL was on the scale of "How to Be."

Then, in eighth grade, I walked into my Advanced English class on the first day of school and met a new girl. She was blonde like me, wore glasses like me, and was an inch taller. Wow, she could be my long-lost twin! She was shy and self-conscious about her height, too.

I recognized the signs because I also hunched my shoulders to appear shorter and slipped away from groups of petite girls to avoid the embarrassment of not being able to hear their whispered conversations because I was a full head taller.

She sat in the back next to me because our order-obsessed English teacher Mrs. Gookins placed everyone in chairs according to our heights. It seemed silly to me because sitting down, we were all more or less the same height, but whatever. It gave me a chance to talk to the new girl, LeEllen. She even had a goofy name, almost as bad as Wilma.

LeEllen (I soon shortened it to Elli) was a shy girl, even more so than me, and she had a very soft voice. Mrs. Gookins, our English teacher, was old and somewhat hard of hearing, so between Elli's soft voice and Mrs. Gookins' fetish about seating tall people in the back of the classroom, you just knew this train wreck was inevitable.

"Speak up, LeEllen! We can't hear you!"

Sitting right next to her, I heard what Elli said perfectly, but I could see Elli shrinking into herself. I could tell she hated that kind of attention but couldn't do much about it. Her naturally soft voice became even softer from fear whenever Mrs. Gookins called on her to speak. When I saw this cruel and unusual punishment, I immediately adopted her as my new best friend.

Elli and I hung out so frequently and looked so much alike, other kids started calling me LeEllen and her Wilma. We corrected them, but really, what difference did it make? If some kids were so unobservant that they couldn't tell us apart, who needed them? It became an unofficial test for new friends who might want to join our small inner circle.

You just called me LeEllen? Uh, no. Go sharpen your skills and try out again next year.

11

Determined to get over our shyness or at least improve, we decided to try out for the school play the following year.

Unfortunately, Mrs. Gookins was the drama teacher, so you can easily imagine how Elli's tryout went when she read the script in her soft voice. She was assigned the role of costume mistress.

My tryout was slightly better. I was given a one-line part. But somehow Mrs. Gookins found out that I had been taking piano lessons for a few years, and she added a piano-playing scene to the play.

I was both terrified and strangely exhilarated when the performance time came. I don't remember much, but I think I did okay.

However, now I was hooked on performing. Shy Wilma. On stage. Who would have guessed?

In tenth grade, a new girl showed up in our Advanced English class, and her name was Tina. Her family had moved to Loveland from a small town in Kansas, so she didn't know anyone. Our compassion took over and Elli and I took her under our wing.

Tina and I hit it off right from the start. We had "friend chemistry." We started spending more time together, while at the same time, Elli started spending more time with a girl named Suzy who lived in the country not far from her. So gradually, Elli and I drifted apart, but remained good friends.

Tina was an extrovert, and we gave each other confidence to try new things. Some of the things we tried were borderline JD (juvenile delinquent), but no one ever suspected us of that kind of behavior because we were at the top of our class scholastically. "Goody Two-Shoes" in appearance, but not factually. It was a good place to be.

Having one successful play performance under my belt, I convinced Tina to join Drama Club with me and try out for a melodrama. To our surprise, we both got parts in the play—I, as an innocent young girl who was taken advantage of by the dastardly villain and Tina as my mother.

We were thrilled to be involved and attended every play practice. By this time, I wore contact lenses, and those thick glasses I hated were in my purse instead of on my face.

That was the beginning of a three-year run of good times. By our senior year, I was the president of Drama Club, and she was the treasurer. We had been involved in all the play productions and musicals, either playing parts or working behind the scenes on makeup or costumes.

We had a membership drive for the Drama Club that year that was so successful, about 25% of the school showed up and wanted to join. I presided over the first meeting, and it was standing room only.

Dear God, thank you for my friends.

-4-

Desperate to Stop Dropping My Fruit Cocktail

◻◇●◇◻

ALTHOUGH THE INSULT about having no personality occurred in grade school, residual doubts about my desirability to boys lingered into high school.

To make matters worse, I tended to get weird around boys I found attractive. Like dribbling down my shirt weird. Or speechless staring weird. Or tripping over thin air and dropping a glass dish of fruit cocktail on the cafeteria floor weird. Twice in ten minutes. In the same spot.

Uh, those are just examples of general weirdness—not MY weirdness. But hopefully, you will understand how I ended up married to someone I considered "practice" until I learned how to talk to boys I liked without spilling fruit cocktail.

Uh... yeah... okay...

It was me.

I dropped the dish. Twice. Broke it both times. But you can see why I needed practice, right?

Christmas break, senior year. Finally! After years of getting gifts my parents thought were suitable—a doll instead of a horse, piano lessons instead of a drum set, lip balm instead of lipstick—I final got a gift I actually asked for. It was a pair of light blue leather ice skates with gray fur trim along the top!

Every year, when the temperature was consistently below freezing, the fairgrounds caretaker would flood the concrete floor in one of the barns, scrape it with a snow shovel, then spray again. He'd repeat the process until a thick layer of ice was built. Then it was opened for business.

Two days after Christmas I borrowed my dad's '65 Ford Galaxie and drove to the fairgrounds. After lacing up my beautiful new skates, I took a spin around the oblong-shaped barn, feeling pretty cute with those fancy skates.

I looked around at the other skaters to see if I recognized anyone. I noticed a boy about my age doing spins on the ice in the center of the barn. I skated around the outer circle and stole looks at him every so often. He wasn't all that cute, certainly not enough to spill a fruit cocktail over, even once.

He apparently worked at the rink this year, because after the first hour, he chased everyone off the ice. Then he started scraping the ice, skating fast and pushing the slush off with a snow shovel in front of him.

He finished quickly, but as I sat in the small annex watching him, an idea took shape.

I'd been thinking of working on my inability to talk to cute boys without losing control of my senses, so why not practice? And why not practice on a boy I *wasn't* attracted to?

The longer I thought about it, the better I liked the idea.

I have to pause here for a minute in this story. I don't recommend doing this, no matter who you are, but particularly not if you have a personality like mine. I have always been sensitive to other people's emotions. As a result, I can grow fond of someone, then be talked into doing something I normally wouldn't because I don't want to hurt their feelings.

Life is too short not to spend it with someone you're crazy in love with, even if you have to push yourself to a whole new level of terrified. It's how you grow. I know that now. But back then I was looking for a shortcut. And my life might have had a whole different trajectory if I hadn't pursued this course.

15

And that's on me.

But I decided to practice on Daryl, the boy at the rink. I thought that flattery surely would break the ice (pun intended), so I complimented his skating ability and asked if he would show me how to do a spin.

We had several short conversations that first day, and I returned to the rink a couple more times that week. Then I said I wouldn't be able to come back for a while because I wouldn't have transportation.

This was only partially true as I could have talked my brother into giving me a ride, but I wanted to see if Daryl would offer to pick me up. He offered, I accepted. My practice was successful on a basic level—I learned how to talk to a boy, although one I didn't find attractive.

Could I now follow through on my ultimate goal and learn how to talk to a cute boy?

After dating for about three months, Daryl invited me to dinner at his house. I met his mother Barbara, along with Donnie and Marie. (Not the Osmonds.) Donnie was Daryl's older brother by five years and Marie was his girlfriend, and they both lived at his mom's house.

Marie had cooked dinner.

Ah, dinner! I was nervous, but I have to state for the record that what happened next was not my fault.

Marie had cooked pigs-in-a-blanket—hot dogs wrapped in dough and baked—with a side order of ketchup. If I'd been at home alone, I would've just picked up the dough-wrapped dog with my fingers and dipped it in the ketchup. But I wanted to make a good impression, so I neatly picked up my knife and fork and started cutting a piece.

The hot dog's little dough blanket was actually a cement encasement, however. The whole dog shot across the table, about eight feet or so, and landed with a clatter on the kitchen floor. It was a great comedic moment.

Except from my perspective, of course. Another episode of food meeting an unhappy fate because of my nerves.

And Marie's lack of cooking skills.

See? Not totally my fault.

But I still died of embarrassment at that moment and was a zombie the rest of the evening. When Daryl took me home afterwards, however, he was the nervous one. He said he wanted to ask me something. He was obviously struggling with it.

I thought he was going to ask me to "go steady," but instead, with many pauses and stuttering starts and stops, he launched into a story about his father. He said his father was a paranoid schizophrenic and had spent quite some time in a mental hospital. His father lived about fifteen miles northwest of Loveland in a trailer in the foothills. His parents were divorced.

Then he got really nervous but finally said what was on his mind.

"After hearing about my father, would you ever consider marrying me?"

After I picked up my jaw from the floor of the car, my brain started racing.

Did he just ask me to marry him?

I'd only known him for three months. How on earth did we turbo-blast from early dating to marriage?

I stuttered with my reply. I don't remember much of what I said, but I do remember the part where I said "yes."

Okay, in my defense, I felt really sorry for him, and he'd only said "consider" marrying him.

If I'd had my wits about me, I wouldn't have said yes. I would have gently said something nice without actually answering the question.

But I said yes, and that moment would become my Waterloo because I absolutely hated to go back on my word or to feel like I had disappointed anyone. I didn't realize how serious my error was at the time, though, because I didn't understand my personality at all back then.

My goal to learn to talk to cute boys fell off the bulletin board and into the waste basket unnoticed.

17

And now I need to give you a little more background about the way things were back then, particularly in Small Town, America. A girl was expected to follow a norm: get married, have children, and spend the rest of her life as a housewife and mother.

If you were too hideous to attract a boy in your teen years, you could pursue one of three occupations: secretary, where you could continue to pursue the ultimate goal of marriage; nurse, where you could sublimate your assumed innate drive to take care of people; or teacher, where you got to take care of other people's children.

My dad wanted me to be a secretary, and my mom thought I would make a splendid English teacher. Neither of these career choices appealed to me.

One could assume that Daryl had asked me to marry him, but he still had one year of high school left since I was one year ahead of him in school. Not knowing what else to do, I studied hard and made plans to attend the University of Colorado in Boulder, postponing any marriage vs. career decisions for one more year.

Dear God, please help me figure out what to do with my life.

□◇●◇□

Is It Just a Game?

A thousand cuts, a thousand choices
every day to make anew.
Am I doomed?
Was I fooled?
In this Game of Life, I wonder,
do I understand the rules?
Can I ever reach the final
goal I'm heading toward?
Can I find a way
to move my token
on this board?

18

Can I find a way
to keep myself
from slipping,
sliding, stalling?
Fear of falling
off the ladder falls upon me as I ponder —
"Which way takes me further, yonder?"
With a head that's filled with questions
and a heart that's filled with fear,
I'm afraid to make a misstep
and afraid to stay right here.
How does anybody know
which way to go?
Which way to be?
To me
it's just a mystery.
Jesus can You help me out
and pull me out of this self-doubt?

-5-

A Scoop of Depression with a Cherry on Top

□◇●◇□

DARYL GAVE ME AN engagement ring on Valentine's Day the year I was in college. We were married the following August.

I tried to convince Daryl that we should both go to college, but Daryl didn't want to go, and to be a "good wife," I didn't go either.

During the fifties and sixties, smart girls were often encouraged to "play dumb." Boys' egos were believed to be too fragile if they found out they weren't as smart or educated as their girlfriends, so I downplayed my intelligence and love of learning back then.

Now I know I was actually lying about who I was. As the months and years went by, I felt like I had to hide many other essential parts of my personality to better fit a traditional female role. I adopted a personality that was more like my mother's—a "June Cleaver" personality.

I didn't grasp until much later the great price I paid for trying to be someone I wasn't.

After the wedding, I found a job as an electronic assembler at the Hewlett-Packard (HP) plant south of town. My job as an electronic assembler was mind-numbingly boring. Every day I dreaded going to work.

After a couple of months of excruciating boredom, I couldn't face going to work anymore, so I came up with a plan.

I would have a baby!

After talking it over with Daryl, I stopped taking birth control pills and immediately got pregnant.

Our precious girl was born with a few strikes against her. Poor Amber. First off, she was tongue-tied. Yes, that's a real thing and not just an expression! Who knew? We sure didn't.

It's an abnormal attachment of the tongue to the floor of the mouth, which prevents a baby from successfully breastfeeding. The doctor corrected it at her ten-day checkup, but by then the damage was done. She had to stop breastfeeding since that wasn't working and go on formula and a bottle.

Unfortunately, she had difficulty digesting the formula and frequently had colic, which was accompanied by ear-splitting screaming most of the night. She slept most of the day so she would have enough energy to scream through the night.

I was the one who got up at night and rocked her, but Daryl still lost a lot of sleep, with an accompanying frequent loss of temper. It was hard.

▫◇●◇▫

Amber was almost a year old when we moved to Denver, fifty miles south of Loveland. The following year we purchased our first home—a small two-bedroom house with a full basement that we planned to finish into a family room, third bedroom, and second bathroom.

Designing the color schemes, making curtains and bed-spreads, hanging wallpaper, and painting the walls—those were tasks I enjoyed. But there were moments when Daryl would yell and curse because something wasn't going right, and it made me cringe. My own father wasn't like that, so I wasn't used to a father behaving that way.

21

I disliked being around Daryl when he lost his temper, but I really hated it when he lost his temper with Amber. She was an extremely sensitive child and was afraid of a lot of things. Instead of being gentle with her, he yelled at her every time she cried for what seemed to him like "no good reason."

He also occasionally spanked her for crying. This only made it worse. Sometimes he yelled at her and spanked her for coughing when she had a cold. These episodes disturbed me greatly, but when I tried talking to Daryl about it, he turned his wrath on me. I started getting bouts of serious depression.

I felt trapped in a no-win situation and was losing hope.

During this time, I wasn't well. I was twenty-one and had spells when I felt light-headed and weak. I fainted and fell one day, and Daryl took me to the hospital. I was okay, but they recommended a five-hour glucose tolerance test.

The test came back, and the doctor told me I had hypoglycemia (low blood sugar). He told me to eat a candy bar or drink orange juice whenever I felt weak or light-headed. I followed his instructions, but it only got worse.

I started researching the condition and found out the best way to treat it was to do the opposite—go on a sugar-free diet, so I tried that next.

To follow the diet as prescribed in the books I read, I had to give up many of my favorite foods or try adjusting recipes. I even made my own versions of sugar-free ketchup and mayonnaise. But the diet didn't help much. I still didn't feel well.

I spent most days in bed and got up fifteen minutes before Daryl came home and pretended I'd been up all day. Eventually I ended up in the hospital again. After hearing my symptoms and running some tests, the doctor recommended that I be admitted to their psychiatric wing.

This was not what I wanted to hear.

I wanted to be told that all my symptoms, depression included, were caused by some easily treatable medical condition. They gave me twenty-four hours to decide. I was hopelessly discouraged and considered taking my own life.

That evening, a sympathetic nurse who had been taking care of me came into my room and shut the door. She told me a story about a woman who had been at the hospital with stomach pains. The doctor decided it was psychosomatic—caused by a mental illness—and put her into the psychiatric ward. She continued to have pain. Eventually it got so bad they brought in a specialist who found out that she had a tumor. They operated, but she almost died because it had taken so long to diagnose.

This kindly nurse recommended that I NOT go into the psych ward because once I was there, I would have a hard time getting out. She was a Christian and recommended that I find a church for counseling instead of staying at the hospital.

So that's what I did. And that's when I met Cherry.

Yes, believe it or not, that was her real name. And the frosting on the cake was her sister, whose name was Peaches!

Cherry befriended me, which was exactly what I needed. She suffered from similar symptoms and found that a balanced diet with minimal sugar (not the drastic diet I was on) worked best for her. She also saw a doctor who treated hypoglycemia with adrenal cortical extract injections, and I started seeing him.

Cherry was a happy, loving, and kind lady in her early thirties who took me under her wing, prayed with me, and showed me that God could answer prayer. I got better, and it was all God's doing. He put the kindly hospital nurse and my friend Cherry into my life to lead me back to Him and save my life, even when I wasn't looking for Him.

With the right medical treatment, Cherry in my life, and a return to church, my depression lifted.

Dear God: Thank you for helping me get better.

-6-

Then There Were Two

I LOVED AMBER MORE than I ever thought possible. She was funny and entertaining and smart. She started talking in complete sentences when she was two and loved to try out new words—especially long ones—with sometimes hilarious results as she tried to fit them into sentences.

When someone said she was "precocious," I later overheard her telling her doll to stop being "pickle-shoes." When I told her to "behave" in the store, she fired back, "I AM being have!"

Amber loved to play "teacher," and she gave complicated instructions to her "students." One day, I overheard her explaining to two teddy bears and a stuffed turtle how to do yarn embroidery. She was using my recently completed and framed embroidered flower basket picture as a prop while she snipped the yarn with small school scissors.

Fortunately, the lesson hadn't progressed very far when I caught her, and only minor damage was done to my handiwork.

◻◇●◇◻

I decided to start a babysitting co-op where parents could exchange babysitting hours with other parents. I left flyers on doorsteps to get the organization started, and it grew significantly after that from word-of-mouth. The ease of finding a

babysitter and the fun of caring for a baby again, albeit someone else's, started me thinking about having another baby. I
talked to Daryl, and he agreed.

This was his second chance to have the boy he wanted.

However, Emily was not a boy. She was a beautiful little girl
with orange hair that quickly fell out and very slowly grew
back in blonde. I got tired of people saying, "Oh, isn't he cute!"
and started taping pink bows on her nearly bald head when I
took her out.

Emily's personality and first year were very different from
Amber's. She had a voracious appetite and grew quickly.
Although she was slender, she was off-the-chart tall for her
age.

People always guessed both her gender and her age wrong.
They thought she was a two-year-old boy when she was a one-
year-old girl.

I loved her tremendously, though, and was secretly thrilled to
have another girl.

□◇●◇□

When Amber was seven, I took her to baton twirling lessons,
and she was surprisingly good at it. Her instructor wanted to
move her to an advanced class after only three lessons.

Amber, however, had other ideas. She said twirling a baton
was boring and she wanted to ice skate. I'd seen her attempts
to ice skate, however, so I tried steering her back to baton
twirling. She would have none of it and insisted on taking ice
skating lessons.

As I sat on the bleachers watching her during her skating lessons, I had the urge to pretend not to know her when other
mothers would ask, "Which one is your child?" It was an easy
answer.

"She's the one that falls down all the time."

Amber loved ice skating and steadfastly resisted all suggestions that she go back to baton twirling. She was the most
resistant, persistent, and stubborn little girl I'd ever seen.

But I had a change of heart when her lessons eventually progressed to jumps and spins. I could see how her persistence paid off. I saw fear on the other children's faces when they tried to do a jump, but only joy on Amber's, even though she fell at least nine out of ten times.

Eventually, though, she started falling only eight out of ten times, then seven out of ten, then six.

When she performed the following year in her first ice show—an energetic set of jumps and spins set to the music "Flight of the Bumblebee"—I was proud of her fierce determination and happy that I'd allowed her to follow her heart.

◻◇●◇◻

When Emily was almost a year old, Daryl was transferred to Colorado Springs. After the transfer, we bought a new house on the north side of the city.

I took Emily to "Mommy and Me" classes at the YMCA when she was about eighteen months old. We did swimming and gymnastics together in the class. She loved it.

I enrolled eight-year-old Amber in skating lessons in Colorado Springs so she could continue training. Emily idolized Amber and wanted to do everything her big sister did. Every so often, I had to run out on the ice to grab Emily before someone skated into her after she'd followed Amber out there like a puppy.

I eventually bought Emily ice skates of her own since the rink didn't rent any for children that young. She took to the ice easily.

I found a good private Lutheran school for Amber. It was free as long as we were church members in good standing. I became involved in the school, often volunteering to serve on committees. I also started giving private piano lessons.

I was busy full-time—carpooling, volunteering, and giving music lessons. Then Amber's ice skating led to an even more serious time commitment when she started entering competitions at the age of eleven. I had to get up at 5:00 a.m. every morning to drive her to the rink so she could practice, then drop her at school and reverse the process in the afternoon.

That long drive every day led me to suggest we find a house closer to the rink.

The house we moved to was about twenty years old and a perfect candidate for remodeling. It was in a great location—much closer to the rink. The grade school was across the street where Emily would be starting kindergarten. Amber would be going to the public junior high school down the street since the Lutheran school only taught grades one through six.

Dear God, thank you for blessing me with a good life and two beautiful girls.

-7-

The Not-So-Chosen People

◻◇●◇◻

AFTER WE MOVED, we started attending the Church of the Open Bible. Now going to church only once a week was a thing of the past.

I started playing the piano in duet with the organist during church services. I co-directed the children's Christmas pageant and made the costumes. We went to Bible study at least twice a week. I was baptized again—this time fully dunked in a mountain lake.

I prayed to be closer to God. I saw how comfortably others led Bible studies, and I wanted to be that articulate and relaxed. I wanted to be able to pray out loud, eloquently and extemporaneously. I wanted God to give me prophetic words to say and to speak in tongues during church services. I longed to have a great conversion story as many others did and have the persuasive oratory skills to tell it properly.

I was still shy, however, and often inarticulate when I merely tried to comment on something we were reading in a Bible study group. Those desires felt like a faraway dream.

Then Daryl lost his job. And it occurred to us that maybe it was a "sign from God."

We decided to sell the house, then use the proceeds to fund Daryl's enrollment into Bible College to become a pastor. We prayed about it. The pastor laid hands on us. The church gave us a going-away luncheon and took up a collection. It was a done deal. God's plan for our lives! Right?

Screeeeeetch!!! Full stop.

Maybe not.

We had an offer on the house, the loan was closing in three days, and we were in the midst of packing when the phone call came. The Realtor explained that the buyer's loan didn't go through. So, no sale, and we would have to start over. Unpack. Clean up the house. Put it back on the market.

Defeated and deflated, we were shell shocked into inaction. We didn't do anything. Except unpack.

I don't remember if we went back to church again. Likely we did at least a few times because not going would have looked worse than quietly fading away.

This is not a moment I am proud of. And my reaction was something I'm even less proud of.

It felt like a monumental betrayal to me at the time. I couldn't figure out why God would trick us. Why would He lead us down a path, only to cause a landslide that swept the ground out from underneath our feet? I was hurt and angry but didn't want to acknowledge either emotion. So, I buried it and rarely spoke about it to anyone.

Until now.

In hindsight, I can think of various comments people could make about what happened, depending on their spiritual leanings and belief or disbelief in God. For example,

#1 "There is no God."

#2 "It was a test of your faith and commitment. You should have proven your commitment by putting your house back on the market."

#3 "You were out of step with God's will. You were more concerned with your own will."

Personally, I choose door #3. After I picked myself up, I tried to forget my shame, embarrassment, and disappointment. I buried it like a bone in the backyard. Now that I've taken it out, shaken off the dirt, exposed it to the light, and examined it, I don't think it was the right path for us.

We—or at least I—fell victim to the idea of being a "force" for God instead of actually seeking God's will and allowing Him to be the force.

I wanted to be Godly. Now I realize that—even more—I wanted to be viewed that way.

My primary motivation was based on what other people thought of me. After things came crashing down, I realized that I was too concerned about the opinion of others, based on how much emotional pain I felt. So here was my new prayer.

Dear God, please help me stop caring so much about what other people think.

God definitely works in mysterious ways, and I soon found out that being refined by fire is not an overstated analogy.

I also realized that I compared myself to others. Depending on my mood at the time, I either came out looking better or worse than the other person. But no matter which way it fell, I was judging others, and in doing so, condemning myself.

There's a good reason God says, "Judge not, lest ye be judged."[3] And I had just found it. There is no winning position in God's eyes when you judge others. And even if you view this principle through a non-religious lens—if you come out feeling better than others or worse than others—it damages your relationships and/or your self-esteem. So I had one more new prayer.

Dear God, please help me stop comparing myself to others.

When It's All Too Much

Too many thoughts to think
opinions to process
clues to decipher

I hang my brain on the clothesline
to flap in the breeze
and bake in the sun

To remove tedious thoughts
odorous opinions
and frayed feelings

Freely it flaps
renews and refreshes
absorbing God's gracious light

-8-

Technically Speaking

_{□◇●◇□}

I WAS THIRTY-TWO when God rejected our bid to serve Him—at least that was how I viewed it at the time. We had some savings, so the income loss from Daryl's layoff wasn't an immediate emergency. However, I still decided to look for a job. I fell back on what I knew and found a job at TRW as an electronic assembler.

At TRW I would be assembling communications modules for the space shuttle program instead of computers as I did in my previous job at Hewlett Packard. It was 1982, and space shuttle events were well-covered by the media, so I was proud to go to work for a company that was involved in the space program.

I was a good assembler. I had excellent dexterity and eye-hand coordination, and my supervisor noticed my good work.

I was soon promoted to senior assembler. This new position meant that I would be working with the test technicians and changing out components that had failed during testing. This process required more skill than the initial build, so only the best assemblers were allowed to work on the completed board modules.

A technician would bring me a plastic tub that contained a module to work on, and after I finished, I carried it back to the technician. In this way, I gradually got to know the eight techs who worked in the back, mostly hidden behind tall racks of test equipment with blinking red lights and flashing green lines.

The whole area was intimidating and fascinating at the same time.

The techs generously answered my questions about what they did—how they tested the equipment. Most of what they said made no sense at the time, but I knew I wanted to know more.

And I started thinking that maybe, just maybe, I could become an electronic technician, too!

One technician was particularly helpful—a man about three years older than me named Jim. When I asked questions about his job, he sometimes lit up as we talked, and he made electronics sound fun. Jim carefully explained what I needed to do if I wanted to become a technician.

Conveniently, there was a tech school just down the road from TRW called Colorado Technical College. I took off during lunch break one day and picked up enrollment forms, completed them, and selected my first course—Basic Electronics.

I looked forward to going to school again. I wasn't sure Daryl entirely approved, but he was busy looking for another job, so I didn't worry too much about it—my desire to learn was too strong.

After one year of school, I convinced the tech supervisor to give me a shot and bring me in as a junior tech. I was ecstatic.

Working in the back of the room was a lot like going back to high school—or maybe junior high. Because the work was incremental and varied in volume, there was a lot of downtime, which I spent studying for my classes and watching the other techs chat, joke, and play tricks on each other.

One day one of the techs attached a latex glove to an air hose and ran it into the back of a rack, while another tech unknowingly worked on a module at the front of the rack. It didn't take long before the expanding glove exploded with a loud pop. The unsuspecting tech ran halfway across the room backward before he realized he had been the subject of another tech's practical joke.

After a few months, I was no longer the new girl and was eligible to be a recipient of their practical jokes.

One day I came back from break, and Jim told me that, while I was gone, Neal, one of the other techs, had swapped out my working spectrum analyzer with one he had that wasn't working correctly and needed to be sent offsite to be fixed. Neal was hoping to see me struggle while I tested a circuit board looking for problems with the board when the problem was in the test equipment.

Jim helped me swap the analyzers back, returning the defective one to Neal's rack while Neal was at break.

After his break was over, Neal stopped by and, with a smirk, asked how my testing was going. "Great!" I responded. He watched for a minute, then went back to his own work.

Out of the corner of my eye, I saw him hook up the defective analyzer to his module and begin the testing process. He frowned, checked the connections, and spent the next thirty minutes trying to figure out what was wrong.

Jim and I couldn't contain our laughter any longer. Then Neal realized what we had done, and the other techs joined in the laughter at Neal's expense.

I felt like I had become "one of them." And it felt good.

Jim always seemed much older than me because he had the aura of someone who had experienced trauma in his life but was also wiser. I jokingly called him Eeyore, the pessimistic donkey—Winnie the Pooh's friend. Jim was also easy to talk to and had a soothing streak of stability and common sense that I appreciated.

His perpetual air of sadness made me want to cheer him up, though, to make him lose the resigned expression he usually wore like a mask. I chatted with him often over the next few months and told him a lot about me, but he told me only basic information about himself.

Eventually he told me about his wife.

She committed suicide. It happened shortly before I started working at TRW. She shot herself in the heart.

Whenever Jim was asked about what had happened to his wife, he always said, "Her heart stopped," and people assumed she had some kind of fatal heart condition.

I finally saw the reason for his world-weary aura. He believed it was his fault.

When I told him it wasn't, he said in a voice tight with emotion, "She obviously didn't want to be with me. We had just gotten married."

I didn't know what to say, but I felt a great deal of compassion for Jim. Our friendship continued to grow.

Dear God, thank you for my job and for my friend Jim.

-9-

The Man Who Believed in Me

◻◇●◇◻

A LOT OF CHANGES occurred in my life the year I turned thirty-three, and I was very grateful that God gave me Jim to talk to.

In early November, my father started having severe back pain and was hospitalized. The doctors determined that the prednisone he'd been taking for years for a skin condition was causing his vertebrae to collapse.

He was somewhat better by Thanksgiving and returned home. Daryl and I took the girls to Loveland for a visit over the Thanksgiving holiday weekend.

That night, my mom woke me and asked me to come into their bedroom. Dad was sitting on the edge of the bed, mumbling about something, obviously confused. Mom showed me his ankle where he'd gotten a bedsore while he was in the hospital.

The sore looked like it wasn't healing. I saw red streaks shooting up his leg. My high school summer job experience as a nurse's aide kicked in.

"Mom. We need to get him to the hospital tonight!"

She wasn't sure it was such an emergency, but I convinced her that the red streaks were a bad sign of infection, and she called for an ambulance since Dad was becoming too difficult to reason with.

Later that night, the doctor told us that we were wise to bring him in so quickly. He had cellulitis, a serious bacterial infection. Dad's mental acuity seemed to be slipping further.

Dad continued to have a few moments of clarity, followed by several hours of confusion. By mid-December, the doctors recommended amputation of his leg just below the knee because the bedsore and accompanying infection had gotten so bad.

My mother called me. "I can't do it," she choked out. "I can't sign the paperwork. George will never forgive me if he wakes up and his leg is gone."

Her heart-breaking sobs, so unusual to hear, strongly affected me. I just wanted to take away her pain.

Without thinking, I said, "I'll do it, Mom."

I later wondered if I would be able to sign the paperwork, but when I thought about my mom's sobs, it strengthened my resolve.

Shortly before Christmas, I made the hundred-mile trip to Loveland so I could sign the paperwork. After I got to Mom's house, however, we got a call from the hospital.

Dad had suffered a stroke.

Mom and I quickly drove to the hospital. He was unable to move his left arm, and that side of his face drooped. He was not coherent. My mom was a wreck, but she hid it fairly well.

The following morning. we went back to the hospital. My mom couldn't bring herself to go in right away, so I went in to visit with Dad a few minutes alone.

He was sitting in a chair with a restraint around his chest so he wouldn't fall out of the chair. He looked at me and opened his mouth, but no words came out.

The nurses had put on his glasses, and the corrective lenses he wore after his cataract surgery made his eyes look large. He had a distressfully sad expression of frustration and helplessness in his oversized eyes that made me want to cry and hug him without stopping.

One hand was curled to his chest, and the other was pounding lightly on the tray in front of him to emphasize his frustration. He had tears in his eyes. I sensed that he wanted to tell me something important but was unable.

It was a heartbreaking sight I will never forget if I live to be a hundred and twenty.

In early January, he had a massive stroke and passed away with both legs intact. He never recovered enough from the first stroke to have surgery. I never had to sign the paperwork.

I was bereft when I learned he had died. My dad was my cheer-leader. He was the one person in my life I could count on to give me confidence. He always applauded my accomplish-ments, even if he didn't quite understand them. He believed in me even if no one else did—even if I didn't.

When I went to Loveland for the funeral, I walked into the foyer and was taken aback to see an open casket right by the doorway into the sanctuary. Dad was lying in it. No, I take that back. There was a deceased body in the casket. But it wasn't Dad. I walked closer. It looked mostly like Dad, but there was something missing. That element that made him my dad. That thing that made him alive and real. It wasn't there.

My dad wasn't in there.

At that moment, I felt an unusual and unexpected peace, knowing that my dad wasn't there but instead was in heaven. My dad was such a faithful believer and a good man, I knew that if anyone were going to heaven, he would be a shoo-in.

In addition to the grief I experienced following my father's death, I was having a hard time "remembering" who I was supposed to be. After staying home for years and behaving like a traditional wife, returning to work was liberating in the sense that my real personality—the one that I'd buried the day I met Daryl—began to slowly emerge.

It was a personality that I'd been only vaguely aware of for the past several years. It was the personality that presided over Drama Club in high school and performed in plays. The per-sonality that loved to laugh and did quirky stunts with Tina while getting top grades. The personality that loved to learn and won numerous awards.

That personality.

After becoming part of the tech group and finding a friend in Jim, I found myself beginning to go home with the same personality I had at work. Daryl didn't recognize it.

But more ominously, he didn't like it.

Dear God, please help Daryl to accept me for who I am.

-10-

The End of Life as I Knew It

DARYL DEVELOPED a new habit of dealing with anger that was worse on my emotional health than his frequent outbursts. Whenever I did something that upset him, he would stop talking to me.

If I asked him what was wrong, he would say, "If you don't know, I'm not going to tell you."

I would spend the next several days obsessing over everything I might have done wrong or should have done and didn't do. I wondered if I was too fat, too thin, or too ugly. I wondered if I'd been abrasive, unfeminine, or forgotten to bury my intellectual capacity. Had I been rude or interrupted when he spoke?

There was no end to the volume of possible errors I might have made.

Then he started including Amber and Emily in this technique. In addition to not speaking to me, he would spend lots of time talking to the girls and ignoring me in an obvious effort to make me feel excluded.

My visible distress only made him repeat the behavior more often because he knew it caused me pain. Now I would call it manipulation and emotional abuse.

A wider chasm between us was the consequence.

I decided to delicately suggest we try marriage counseling. I was still trying to think of a way to approach the subject when one day my honest feelings spilled out before I had a chance to reconsider or rephrase the statement.

"I feel like you don't love me anymore."

I don't remember how he responded, but it wasn't reassuring. I mentioned marriage counseling, and the topic made him leave the room.

I decided to go to counseling anyway and found a therapist who was on my health plan. I liked her. After I saw her every week for a couple of months, Daryl finally broke down and agreed to go, too.

The first couple of sessions were uneventful, but in the third session, Daryl started complaining about my friendship with Jim. In the fourth session, he dropped a bomb.

What Daryl said next hit me like a charging bull moose.

He told me he'd had an affair six years before. And that the only reason he was telling me now was to save me from making the same mistake with Jim that he'd made years ago with a woman in his office.

It was a good thing I was firmly planted in my chair, or I would have fallen on the floor. They say in cases like this, the wife always has clues and should know. In my case, however, my first impulse was to ask,

Are you SURE?

At first, I took what Daryl said at face value. I wanted to believe that he still loved me and really just wanted to save me from—what? From guilt? From myself?

From what, exactly?

In a later counseling session, I wanted to explore this topic, which made Daryl walk out of the therapist's office and never return. Before long I realized something that my therapist confirmed. Daryl's primary motive was not to "save me," it was to hurt me.

41

To me, marriage was a sacred vow.

I believed in the promise, "'til death do you part." I believed that God allows divorce in the case of unfaithfulness, but not much else as long as a life is not in danger. I believed that my commitments were an important part of who I was.

After the shock of Daryl's revelation wore off, my attitude toward him changed. I wasn't totally devastated. I wasn't unbearably hurt. I wasn't completely destroyed. I wasn't even angry—well, maybe I was at least a little angry. But I have to admit that my primary feeling was relief.

Yes, oddly enough, relief.

The only anger I felt wasn't for the deed itself. No, I was angry because I'd wasted years staying married to someone with a strong streak of cruelty toward both the kids and me when I was, in God's eyes, entitled to a divorce.

Then I thought about it some more and realized that when the infidelity occurred, divorce wasn't practical anyway. I had no income of my own, and if the divorce had occurred right after Emily was born, it would've been difficult to manage my life with a six-year-old, a newborn baby, no husband, and no income.

Then I did the only thing that felt right at the time: I moved out of the bedroom and into the guest room. I had to decide if I really wanted a divorce.

In the meantime, Daryl started alternating his tactics—yelling at me one day to straighten up and start acting like "a wife" again and the next day, giving me flowers to apologize.

Dear God, please forgive me for believing I needed a husband to survive and be whole when I should have depended on you. And please guide me now.

-11-

Cartwheels Down the Stairs

□◇●◇□

ONE DAY DARYL brought home divorce papers written by a lawyer and asked me to sign them. I took them with shaky hands.

This was now a whole new level. Once my mind accepted that this was the new reality, I got my own lawyer and proceeded to revise them.

When I handed the signed papers back to Daryl a week or so later, he looked surprised, took the papers, and tore them up. He said he didn't really want a divorce. He was just trying to make me see how serious this was so I would come to my senses.

Hearing this was just one more ploy to manipulate me gave me just the resolve I needed not to cave in. I didn't change my behavior. I kept my job and made no attempts to go back to the June Cleaver housewife that Daryl wanted.

My stress level was high, but I had to be faithful to the personality inside me that wanted to live again.

I talked about it a lot with Jim, my friend at work, and he helped me pull myself and my emotions back together again. His kindness toward me and the girls made me realize that I could have a life without Daryl's manipulation and cruelty hanging over my head—the trade-off for the security of being in this marriage.

I also continued to go to counseling. She helped me identify the real issues—especially those that were my fault—so I could address them before I dragged them into another relationship.

She suggested I start a journal and make a list of what I wanted in a relationship. At the top of the list I wrote, "I want to be understood and appreciated for who I am and not be expected to be someone I'm not." I also wrote a promise to myself to never again become monetarily dependent on a man if I could help it.

I wrote in the journal daily, and it helped steady my tumultuous emotions.

A few weeks later, on October second—my thirty-fourth birthday—I came home from work to a surprise.

Barbara, Daryl's mother, was sitting in my rocking chair. Daryl was standing next to her smiling—no, it was more of a smirk—and I immediately saw that half the furniture was missing. I looked in the kitchen and half of the contents were missing. I looked upstairs and ALL the bedroom furniture was missing.

I went back downstairs, furious that he'd removed whatever he wanted without talking to me about it. The fact that it was also my birthday felt like a purposeful slap in my face.

I looked at Barbara sitting in the chair and angrily said, "So, you helped him with this?" She just smiled sheepishly, and Daryl handed me new divorce papers.

I eagerly accepted them.

We needed to tell the girls we were getting a divorce, although I was sure they knew what was going on. I no longer slept in the master bedroom, and the cold waves coming at me from Daryl could turn boiling water into icicles. We didn't formally say anything to them about it until the following Saturday.

Daryl and I decided it was better if we had joint custody. The girls would live with me during the week and visit him every other weekend. We sat down with them and told them what would happen.

Both the girls had little visible reaction to the news, which I realized was not reflective of their actual feelings. They'd become adept at hiding their emotions since Daryl didn't like it when they displayed any.

I resolved to have a heart-to-heart talk with each girl alone so they could express their feelings and talk them out with me.

About thirty minutes after revealing the pending divorce, I was in the kitchen making a late lunch when I heard a couple of bumps, then hysterical screaming. I ran into the living room. Emily was sitting on the floor, holding her arm out in front of her, looking at it and screaming.

I saw her arm, but at first, I couldn't comprehend what I was seeing. Her arm appeared to be bent a few degrees in the middle of the forearm, where I knew there wasn't a joint.

It shouldn't look like that.

It finally dawned on me that Emily had broken her arm, and it was bad, judging from the angle of her arm. I winced and cringed in empathetic pain.

Emily was my baby.

I called for Daryl, who was out in the garage, and asked Emily what had happened. Stuttering and sobbing uncontrollably, she said, "I fell down the stairs."

Daryl started the car, and I helped Emily get in without jostling her arm. We sped to the nearest hospital.

That evening after we made it home from the emergency room with Emily's arm in a special type of cast, Amber came into my room and said, "Mom, Emily has something she wants to tell you."

Emily was crying softly behind Amber and seemed very reluctant to talk. Amber said, "Go on, Emily. Tell Mom how you really broke your arm."

After sobbing loudly for a few more minutes, Emily finally choked out, "I was doing cartwheels."

"You were doing cartwheels in the living room?"

She continued sobbing and finally said, "No, I was doing them..."

She said it so softly, I didn't understand. I asked her to repeat.

She blurted out, "Amber, would you?"

Amber said firmly, "She was doing cartwheels down the stairs, and her arm hit the wooden rocker when she landed."

I gaped at her. "You were doing WHAT? Cartwheels?? Down the STAIRS?!"

Amber said, "She didn't want to say because Dad always yells at her for doing cartwheels in the house."

I tried to calm my emotions and sighed. It was a good rule. No cartwheels in the house. At the time, I didn't fathom the need to add, "and especially not down the stairs!"

If Daryl found out, he would hit the roof, and the last thing Emily needed just then was her dad yelling at her.

"Are you going to tell Dad?" Emily timidly asked.

"It's ok, Emily. I won't say anything this time and you learned your lesson. You won't try that again, right? Once was enough to know that it's a terrible idea to do cartwheels down the stairs."

She started sobbing again, then softly said, "Four times."

"Four... what??"

"It was my fourth time down the stairs. I landed the first three times and didn't fall."

Dear God, please help us make it through this change in our lives.

-12-

Starting Over Newly Hatched

◻◇●◇◻

WE SPENT THE NEXT few months negotiating terms. I still couldn't believe I was going through a divorce. I was busy getting the house ready to sell and finding a place for the girls and me to live. Emily was seven at the time and Amber had just turned fourteen.

When the time came for me to talk with Amber about the divorce and how she felt about it, I could see she was really struggling with it. She bit her lip, started to speak, and stopped.

Then she forcefully said, "If you hadn't gotten a divorce soon I was going to run away from home."

"Oh honey!"

Her throat seemed to tighten, and her voice was squeaky and loud at the same time.

"I just couldn't take Dad anymore!" she said, but the last word was more like a wail as she broke down in tears.

I hugged her and said, "Things will get better, honey. I promise. We'll move into a new place—just the three of us. And things will get better."

Eventually things settled down. I sold the house, and the girls and I moved into a three-bedroom apartment. The divorce was final the following April. When it was Daryl's weekend to have the girls over, Emily went without a fuss, but there were times when Amber couldn't be persuaded to go at all, no matter what I said.

Jim was a solid rock through the whole process and helped me at every turn. He even gave us ducks.

One day, Amber came home from school with a chicken egg that had been partly incubated. Each class member had been given one and was expected to dissect them. Amber didn't want to do that and talked the biology teacher into allowing her to bring it home and complete the incubation process, but we didn't have an incubator.

I suspected that Jim would know where we could borrow one, and I wasn't wrong. His mother had one stored in her barn, and before that fetal chick knew it, a new home had been set up just for him—or her.

In due course, the chick hatched. For a week we enjoyed watching him—or her—just peeping and eating and growing. Then one day, he—or she—stiffened up and died. Jim said that sometimes chicks have heart attacks. Sadness ensued, but Jim came to the rescue again, this time with six duck eggs ready for the incubator.

Amber carefully took the eggs and placed them into the incubator. She patiently listened while Jim explained how she would need to sprinkle water on the eggs and turn them every few hours to simulate the way the parental ducks cared for them.

She evidently heard and followed his instructions perfectly because all six eggs hatched! We watched the ducklings grow, and before long, we saw that we had one female duckling and five males. Amber and Emily named them Daisy, Daffy, Donald, Huey, Dewy, and Louie.

It wasn't long before we realized that keeping six ducks in an apartment wasn't a great idea, so it was time to say good-bye, and they went to live with Jim's mother. We visited them a few months later, and they were enjoying a swim in his mother's small pond.

By August, I was ready to try the Divorce Recovery Workshop I'd heard advertised on the radio. It was at a large

Presbyterian Church in downtown Colorado Springs. My introverted nerves kicked in, and I almost didn't go. Then I remembered a quote by e.e. cummings, "It takes courage to grow up and become who you really are."

They assigned the attendees—there were about a hundred of us—to small groups to meet for the rest of the six-week workshop. As I was walking to my assigned classroom, I heard someone close behind me. I turned and saw with a shock that it was Daryl! He was smirking when he told me that he also decided to attend and was assigned to the same small group.

I promptly left. The following week, I went to the Methodist Church on the north side of Colorado Springs and signed up for their Divorce Recovery Workshop.

Dear God, please give me peace during this stressful time.

◻◇●◇◻

Feelings

I've been happy, I've been sad
I've been fearful, I've been mad.
But, in spite of how I feel,
I try to take the time to kneel
and ask You to create in me
a heart that's clean,
a spirit right,
a soul that's free
to praise tonight,
even if my skies were gray
—in spite of how I felt today—
with thoughts that tried to steal away
my peace while I was in the fray.
I'll not think of yesterday—
Close to You is where I'll stay.

-13-

Day One of the Best of My Life

◻◇●◇◻

THE YEAR IS 1985, six weeks short of my thirty-fifth birthday. Late summer, hot and dry. Outside the window, the grass is gasping for water. This is my first time in the Single's Group Sunday school at Calvary Methodist Church, and I don't yet know anyone. I glance up as the hallway door opens for the third time in five minutes, and a tall man walks in.

I turn my attention back to Ruth, the class leader. She has been talking about the class schedule for fall.

Ruth's voice is interrupted by scraping noises.

With a grin resembling that of a small boy caught in a minor infraction, the latest newcomer, somewhere in his mid-thirties with very dark brown hair and light brown eyes, is noisily opening a metal folding chair. He seems unconcerned about the disturbance he is creating.

He catches me watching him and smiles. The skin around his honey-colored eyes creases into a roadmap of wrinkles—evidence of a frequent usage of smile muscles.

The class progresses, and I'm having trouble concentrating. I wonder if the tall newcomer has been here before. I've been coming to the church's Divorce Recovery Workshop for weeks, but this is my first time in a Sunday school class.

The class is over. I find myself walking down the staircase just behind the tall newcomer. I try to think of something clever to say, something to make those riveting eyes shift toward me, but I can't think of anything. I watch my beige sandals descend the staircase, step-by-step. I finally reach the last step and look up, but it's too late.

He's gone.

That evening, I sit in my apartment with the textbook for my technical writing class in my lap. Instead of studying, I'm thinking about the Sunday School class that morning and the tall newcomer. During class, when it came time for introductions, he said his name was Clark. Clark's energetic enthusiasm seemed extraordinary.

My energy level has long since diminished to a slow drip. I've become so used to observing instead of doing, I don't know how to be any other way. People say my quiet demeanor is soothing, but from where I sit, it only seems boring.

No haunting dreams, dark premonitions, or vague forebodings troubled me the day I met Clark. I close my eyes and see him again, slipping quickly and cleanly into my life like a knife into a well-baked custard.

◻◇●◇◻

The Singles' Group holds informal get-togethers about once a week. Clark attends nearly every one of them, and I've had a chance to chat with him several times. He adds an electric charge to the group—he's intelligent and funny, with a sense of humor that teeters on the edge of outrageous.

Tonight, I'm on my way to a Singles' Group spaghetti supper. While I drive, my mind drifts to Daryl and the relationship we had. It was one of dependency—a symbiotic relationship between two insecure people cemented together by mutual shyness and commonality of one overarching trait. We both worried excessively about what other people thought of us.

I only recently came to understand these facets of our personalities. Going to counseling both before and after the death of our marriage was extraordinarily painful. I understand now how my weaknesses contributed to the failure of our marriage.

51

I felt insecure about myself from the day Daryl and I met.

Because of that insecurity, I'd begun mimicking more traditional personality traits that were like my mother's. Daryl seemed to admire that type, but it wasn't me. I was only just now beginning to find out who I was as an adult.

A quote by Bernard Malamud, who wrote the book *The Natural,* drifts into my head.

> *We have two lives — the life we learn with and the life we live after that.*

It was easier to blame Daryl's faults. But it was my own insecurities that led me into a relationship I should never have entered. It was like being punched in the face when I finally saw the truth.

This is not to say that I'd overcome my tendency to worry about what other people thought.

No, I was still fighting that battle.

By the time I find the address for the spaghetti supper, the street is already lined with cars, and I have to park almost a block away. The house belongs to one of the Singles' Group members, and it's packed with people.

I find myself scanning the faces of the guests, looking for Clark. I don't see him. The depth of disappointment I feel surprises me.

I turn to the buffet table, pile some food on a plate, and find a place to sit on the sofa, wedged between Ruth, the Sunday School class leader, and a man I hadn't met before.

The man tells me his name is Lawrence and that he's a lawyer. He is tall and lanky — like Clark. I smile and respond, but my mind is still recovering from disappointment over Clark's absence.

After Lawrence finishes his plate of spaghetti, he stands up and tells no one in particular that he is going to the kitchen for seconds.

"Can I bring you something?" he politely asks me. I decline.

I feel ashamed of my distracted attitude and silently scold myself for being so disheartened about the absence of a man I barely know. Then I look up and Clark is standing in front of me with his ever-present grin.

"Anyone sitting here?" he asks, as he sits down on the sofa where Lawrence had been sitting a moment before. He's balancing a plate of spaghetti in one hand and a Coke in the other. I glance toward the buffet table and see Lawrence's head above the crowd. He's talking animatedly and appears to be engrossed in the conversation.

"You are," I tell him with a smile.

Dear God, thank you for helping me start over.

-14-

How I Stopped Being Someone Else

◻◇●◇◻

I'M SURPRISED AND vaguely alarmed at the pleasure I feel now that Clark is sitting on the sofa beside me at the Singles' Group spaghetti supper. I can't stop smiling, and I hope he won't realize that it's solely because of his presence.

"Well, it's official," I cryptically remark to both Clark and Ruth, as I sit sandwiched between the two of them on the sofa.

"What is?" Clark asks between bites.

"You can't call me Wilma anymore. My official, legal name is now Susan. I got my paperwork from the court yesterday."

A few weeks before, during one of our Sunday School classes, the conversation had somehow drifted to the subject of names. I mentioned that I'd never felt like a "Wilma," even though it was my real name. Eventually, I told the whole story about how I learned in kindergarten that my name wasn't really Susie, that it was just a nickname. I also told them how my teacher insisted on calling me Wilma because there was a Susan in the class already.

Right away, Ruth, the class leader who'd become a friend by then, started calling me Sue and encouraged me to have it changed legally.

It had never occurred to me before that moment— the thought that I could bury Wilma, once and for all.

"You mean you really did it?" Clark responds.

"I did. Something happened at work that made me decide to change it legally."

"They were going to fire you because people named Wilma can't work at TRW?" he asks with mock seriousness.

"No. They..."

"You found out that only people named Susan get promoted?" he teasingly continues.

"No!"

"They told you that your..."

I interrupt with feigned exasperation, "Shut up and listen! Don't you want to hear this?"

"Of course, I do. Stop stalling around and tell me," he says with a grin.

"It sounded so wonderful, being called Sue again instead of Wilma," I tell Clark, "that I decided to have my identification badge at work changed. I went to Security and told them I wanted my badge retyped. Lynn, the woman who works in that department, asked me why. I told her the whole story, but she said she couldn't change it. She said 'company policy' prevented them from putting anything but legal names on ID badges.

"Then I said, 'What about Bob or Dick instead of Robert or Richard? You put those nicknames on badges.' She told me those were legitimate nicknames, but mine wasn't because Sue isn't short for Wilma. I was beginning to get mad. I guess it brought back memories of kindergarten and how I felt back then that my name had been stolen. So I left, and on the way out I said, 'I'll be back. And you WILL be retyping my name.'"

Then I pull out my new ID badge and gleefully dangle it in front of his nose.

"See this?" I triumphantly demand. It reads *Susan Dickinson.*

I don't mention that the other techs good-naturedly teased me about my name change the first day, calling me Wilma Sue until they had squeezed all the fun they could out of the joke. I didn't care. My name is now Susan legally, and it's exciting!

Ruth asks, "What does your mom think about it?"

"She wasn't thrilled," I respond. "But she said she guessed she'd have to get used to it again."

Several years ago, my brother David married a woman named Susie, and for the first time in my life, my family stopped calling me Susie and started calling me Wilma. To prevent "confusion," they said, but it was the final death blow to my identity. Even Daryl had called me Wilma.

"No one can call me Wilma again," I tell Ruth with satisfaction. "My sister-in-law is a little unhappy, though, now that I've taken 'her name.'"

Overhearing our conversation, Clark interjects, "You can tell her that 'Wilma' is available now."

Root beer dribbles down my chin as I struggle to keep my laughter in check.

During the drive home, I am still smiling. Just before I left, Clark asked me to go skiing with him and other members of the Singles' Group the day after Thanksgiving. He said I had to go, that it was "tradition." I told him I didn't know how to ski.

"You mean you've never skied before?" he asked.

"Never."

"And how long did you say you've lived in Colorado?"

"All my life."

I frequently had to defend my inability to ski.

"People from other states foolishly assume that Coloradoans were born with skis on their..." I began.

"Good," Clark had interrupted. "I like to teach people to ski. It gives me an excuse to ski backwards."

"I'll have to bring my kids. My ex is going to be out of town that day."

"The more, the merrier. I'll teach them how to ski, too."

Before I left the party, he made me promise to go. He was so enthusiastic and reassuring that my fear of trying to learn to ski started shrinking. His excitement was contagious.

I am excited, too, but as I turn into my apartment's parking lot, I realize that my own excitement has less to do with skiing and more to do with Clark.

□◇●◇□

"Cheer up."

A familiar voice breaks into my reverie. I look up from the mesmerizing, hill-shaped green trace redrawing itself on my test equipment. Jim, my work buddy, is standing there watching me.

"You going to break?" Jim asks. He's always very punctual about taking coffee breaks—and everything else.

I sigh. "I guess so."

I get up from my test bench and walk with him to the cafeteria.

Jim orders and pays for his usual cup of coffee, and I pick out a frozen dessert. As I nibble around the edges of my ice cream sandwich, I introduce a new subject.

"Amber's got a new boyfriend. He's a year older than she is— a junior at Fountain Valley. I haven't met him yet, but she seems to like him a lot. They're working on a project together at school."

"Uh oh," Jim responds pessimistically. You'd better watch out. "You're going to be a grandmother before you know it."

I make a face. "You'd better be wrong, Eeyore. I'm much too young to be a grandmother."

After a pause, I continue. "We were invited to go skiing the day after Thanksgiving, but Amber wants to stay here. She's supposed to go to a movie with Marty, her new boyfriend, and she's afraid we won't get back in time."

"Skiing, huh?" he says inquisitively. He knew I'd never skied. He hadn't either. We always figured we were the only two people born in Colorado who'd never skied.

"Yeah. With a guy I met a few weeks ago. He goes to my church."

I know I'm opening the door for more teasing from the other techs, but I want to talk to someone about it, and Jim is good at keeping his mouth shut.

"Sounds serious," he comments.

"I don't know. He seems to think he can teach me to ski. He's always cracking jokes and he's really fun to be around, but he hasn't actually asked me out yet. The ski trip is with a group."

I decide to continue.

"The weird part is, a couple of months ago, I was talking with my neighbor about our 'ideal man.' Hers was a tall blond cowboy from Texas, but I said my ideal guy was from Boston and was tall, dark, and handsome. Clark is six-three. And guess where he grew up."

I pause for effect.

"In Boston. And that conversation with my neighbor happened before I ever met him. I just thought it was an interesting coincidence."

Jim just shakes his head, Eeyore-style, which makes me laugh.

Dear God, please continue walking beside me.

-15-

Perfect is a Lonely Peak

◻◇●◇◻

THIS EVENING I'M studying for my tech writing class when the phone rings.

"Hello," a male voice says cheerfully. "I'm calling to check the temperature of your feet."

"My what?" I ask, bewildered.

"Your feet. Have you developed cold feet about skiing yet?"

I laugh. It's Clark. "Not yet. But maybe you should reconsider whether you want to undertake such an impossible project."

"I learned how to ski in less than a day. It probably won't take you even half that long. I'll start you out on the bunny slope, then after lunch, we'll go up to the top and ski down—it's green all the way."

To the top? That sounds a little scary.

"What does green mean?" I ask.

He explains the color-coding system for designating the difficulty of ski slopes. He also suggests I buy some waterproof ski pants so if I fall, I won't get wet and cold. Since wet and cold are two of my least favorite conditions, I mentally make a note to purchase a pair.

"How's your project going?" he asks me.

I'd mentioned my tech writing project during a previous Singles' Group outing. It's a proposal to give training to the assemblers to reduce the number of errors they make.

I update him on my progress, then he remarks, "You really should start going to a real school."

"I do go to a real school. It costs real money."

'Why don't you go to UCCS?" he asks. I knew that he worked for and attended classes at the University of Colorado in Colorado Springs.

"Because they don't have the courses I want to take," I respond defensively.

I'm afraid he's getting too close to the truth about my education, and I try to steer him off the topic. It doesn't work. He smells subterfuge. We continue to debate, but he won't give up. I try to change the subject.

"Where did you ski when you lived back East?" I ask him innocently.

"Why are you trying to change the subject?" he counters.

I sigh. The guy is sharp. I don't know if I resent his nosy questions or appreciate his interest in my life.

"I used to go to school at CU in Boulder." UCCS was the Colorado Springs campus of the University of Colorado. "I went to school there for a year, right after high school."

"Then why didn't you just transfer to UCCS?"

I hesitate for a long moment.

"Because my grades aren't good enough." I say with shame.

"How bad are they?"

Will he never give up?

"Not good," I respond vaguely.

"Did you have less than a 2.0 average?"

"No." I shudder.

"Then what?"

I'm silent. I know he won't understand.

"Well? I'm waiting..."

Jerk. He has me cornered.

"I had a 3.1 average," I say bitterly.

A B average?" he asks with astonishment. "A B? What's so bad about a B?"

I was sick for weeks with mononucleosis when I went to CU and couldn't complete all the required work, but I don't tell him that. It sounds too much like a convenient excuse for not doing well.

"I have a straight A average at Colorado Tech."

"Are you saying that because you didn't get straight As at CU, you won't go to UCCS?" he asks in apparent disbelief.

" You know they'll average my grades, and even if I get straight As from now on, by the time I graduate, I will never get above a 3.75. That's not good enough for me. Since Colorado Tech isn't part of the CU system, they don't include grades from other colleges so I should be able to graduate with a 4.0 GPA."

I'm not proud of my perfectionist streak and I hate discussing it. But he pushes me to talk about it, and I am irritated by the embarrassment the discussion is causing me.

"When God was passing out tact, you must have been out to lunch," I say with feeling.

He just laughs. He's getting a real kick out of my discomfort.

"If I had a 3.1 average, just once in my life, my mother would die of heart failure."

"So, what's your GPA now?" I ask, still not placated.

"I have about a 2.3," he responds. "So, you're way ahead of me."

I'm silent. I know lots of people don't get straight As, but I'm so used to defining my worth in concrete terms like grade point averages, I have a hard time imagining how it would feel to be different. I try to put myself in his place. What would it be like to still feel okay about yourself when you only had a 2.3 average?

I know I probably sound arrogant to him, and I also know that most people aren't such perfectionists and don't worry so much about what other people think of them.

Clark is definitely like that, and I'm drawn to it. I suffer a lot of agony because of my pride and often wish I were different. I avoid trying anything new because I'm afraid, not of outright failure, but of a less-than-perfect performance. As a result, I've been lingering in the gray-toned world of low-risk choices and predictable outcomes. Like my first marriage.

I feel exposed, almost naked. My face feels hot and I'm sure I'm blushing.

"So, what other terrible secrets do you have?" he asks cheerfully.

"Absolutely none," I say decisively.

He's still curious and won't let up. One question leads to another. Even though he dragged an embarrassing secret out of me, I still answer his other questions with as much honesty as I can, although I can't say why. Something about him makes me open the book of my life and let him read it.

God, please help me learn how to become less of a perfectionist.

The Gift

So often, we don't know
how others might view us.
Sometimes it just seems
they're seeing right through us.
All our disguises
and compromises
are all illusions
that cannot excuse us.

What we all need
is for someone to choose us,
someone who sees us,
whose presence renews us,

who sees who we are
—more clearly by far—
and tells us about
all the things that elude us.

They are the mirrors
that give us a view
of traits that we have,
but haven't a clue.
They are pure gold
—like treasure untold—
true friends that reflect
back to us what is true.

You were the gift
I thought was unneeded.
You were the truth
that, at long last, succeeded
in making me see
the reality
of what I am worth
and have been since birth.

-16-

Living Life in Living Color

□◇●◇□

THE RED DIODES on my digital clock read three a.m. I've been talking to Clark on the phone for *six hours!* My ear feels like a dried-up cantaloupe.

"How's your ear?" I ask. "Mine feels like it's about to fall off."

"Mine too. Hey! Do you like chocolate milk?"

Yeah," I answer. "I love chocolate anything."

"Do you have any milk?"

I think for a second. I'm pretty sure Emily finished it off at supper, but for some reason, I don't want to say no. "I think so," I tell him.

"Great. I'll be over in ten minutes. I'm going to make you the best chocolate milk you ever had."

I watch for his car. I don't want him to ring the doorbell and wake the girls. They would undoubtedly wonder why their mother is having visitors at three a.m. I even wonder myself.

Something serious has happened to my usual, gray-toned world—it's being painted with a broad stroke of bright and cheerful color called Clark.

He has a blender in one hand and a can of powdered chocolate drink mix in the other. I lead him to the kitchen and open the refrigerator. My hunch was right. No milk. I try to make light of it.

"I have powdered milk. Will that do?"

"No, it has to be real milk. How could you persuade me to come all the way over here, luring me with a promise of chocolate milk, when all the time you were out of milk!" he complains.

Then I see him looking beyond me, into my open cupboard. He moves in close, reaches into the cupboard, and pulls out a can of hot cocoa mix. I watch as he starts making hot cocoa instead of the chocolate milk he had planned.

We sit on my old green sofa and drink our hot cocoa. On the phone he'd asked dozens of questions about my childhood, my former marriage, and my opinion about everything under the sun. Now it's my turn. I ask him all the questions I can think of. Sometimes he balks and tries to make a joke or change the subject.

However, one event that he recounts makes me laugh so hard I have to clamp both hands over my mouth to keep my laughter from waking the girls.

When Clark lived in Massachusetts, he and a couple of buddies were in Bellows Falls, Vermont, when Clark's transmission malfunctioned, and the car would only go in reverse. Unable to find a mechanic in Bellows Falls, he made an appointment at the nearest repair shop twenty-two miles away in New Hampshire.

Not wanting to pay for a tow, Clark told his buddies to hop in the car, and being young and foolish, they obeyed and watched with a combination of fascination and fear as Clark drove his car in reverse to the highway connecting the two towns.

Other travelers gaped when they saw a young man driving at near-highway speed down the road backwards. However, none had the opportunity to express an opinion until Clark was stopped backwards at a stoplight. His right turn signal was on, indicating his intention to turn left when the light changed.

The man in the lane next to Clark rolled down his window and called out helpfully, "Did you know that you're driving backwards?"

By the time the black night turns soft gray, I feel like I know Clark very well and have known him for a long time. Clark's story about his car being stuck in reverse still lingers in my mind as I think of how "stuck in reverse" is a perfect metaphor for my life. Until now.

He smiles at me and walks to his car, waving good-bye. Although only grayness surrounds him now and no moon shines over the strip of lawn, I feel like Dorothy stepping out of a black-and-white Kansas landscape into a technicolor whirl of drama and excitement in the land of Oz.

Dear God, thank you for creating this astoundingly beautiful, colorful world.

-17-

A Norman Rockwell Thanksgiving

□◇●◇□

DURING OUR MARATHON evening together, I'd learned a lot of things about Clark. His previous marriage lasted five years, and he is thirty-four—nine months younger than me. His father is deceased, and his mother lives in Colorado Springs. His sister, her husband, and their son also live in the Springs, and Clark lives with them.

He said I reminded him of his sister, Wanda. When he followed up with, "She's really crazy, but you'll like her," I wasn't sure what to think.

One day, Clark calls and invites me to Thanksgiving dinner at his sister's house.

I accept. When he finds out that I still need ski wear for our trip the day after Thanksgiving, Clark offers to take me shopping.

Shopping with Clark is a unique experience. He doesn't have "store behavior" like I do. I'm always conscious of an audience.

Clark, on the other hand, has fun. He takes me to display after display, picking up items of ski clothing and jamming them on my hand or head. Huge gloves, oversized hats—he dresses me like his personal Barbie doll, then stands back to admire his handiwork.

He never notices when salespeople approach, but when I see one heading in our direction, I stop giggling. I quickly put on my public face and peer at them through the ski mask or goggles that Clark, just seconds before, had slipped on my head.

I respond to their sudden presence with a polite, "No thank you, we're just looking."

As they walk away, Clark reverts to previous antics. He adds one more article of clothing—a sock on my hand—and leads me to a mirror where I can appreciate the full effect.

Despite the horseplay, I go home with satisfactory purchases—a baby-blue waterproof ski suit, a knitted hat with white fake fur trim, warm gloves, and tinted goggles.

And the store personnel breathe a sigh of relief.

On Thanksgiving Day, Clark picks me up at eleven o'clock and drives me to his sister's house. She is tall and has dark brown hair like Clark's. But unlike Clark's honey-colored eyes, hers are dark brown.

"I didn't realize you were coming," she says. "But we have plenty of food, so don't worry about that. Clark can introduce you to everybody."

She smiles with a distracted air, and I can tell that the future success or failure of dinner is uppermost in her mind.

Clark leads me into the family room, a homey den with a red brick fireplace at the far end. A lanky teen-aged boy, engrossed in playing a large arcade-style video game absentmindedly says, "Hi, Uncle Clark."

A short man who'd been watching the game turns toward Clark. He reminds me of Snow White's famous dwarf, Doc, with a scruffy beard and gold-rimmed glasses.

"Well, Clark, who is this?" he asks with a smile.

"Sue, this is Russ, my sister's husband, and Bill their son," Clark says and then disappears for a moment. He returns with a small green parrot perched on his shoulder. "And this is Gus."

He turns his head toward the bird, puckers his lips and makes a faint smacking sound. The bird cocks its head and lightly picks at Clark's lips. It looks as though they're kissing.

"Clock!" I hear someone call out. I turn around and see white, shiny angel hair framing the face of an older woman who has features that remind me of both Clark and his sister.

"Hi, Mum," Clark says as he bends over to plant a kiss on a fragile white cheek. "This is Sue. I picked her up off the side of the road and she looked hungry, so I brought her with me."

"Don't pay any attention to him," she says to me as Clark coaxes the bird onto her shoulder. "Clock doesn't know how to introduce people properly." She says it affectionately, and her thick Boston accent is lyrical, but I have to listen closely to understand what she is saying.

"I'm helping Wander in the kitchen," she says. "Clock, you'd better set up the cod table."

Vaguely wondering what a cod table was, I trail after Clark into the dining room. I watch him slide out a small square table, unfold the legs, and set it upright.

Then it dawns on me—card table, that's what she'd said. Card table.

"What happened to your accent?" I ask Clark. "It's almost gone."

'When I was in the sixth grade, my family moved to Texas for a year. I had to lose it."

I pictured a young Clark, freshly arrived from Boston, surrounded by a group of mocking twelve-year-old Texans.

Yes, I could see what he meant.

But he hadn't completely lost his accent. Once or twice, I'd heard him ask a waitress for a "strawer" for his Coke.

During the next hour, an assortment of people, both adults and children, arrive. As dinner time nears and the turkey and ham are pulled from the ovens picture-perfect, Wanda seems more relaxed.

In many ways, she reminds me of Clark, although she is three years older. I can tell that both he and his sister have spent long years perfecting the art of sibling rivalry with good-natured bickering and insults.

Two hours later, overstuffed from eating so much food, I sit at the table just listening to the laughter and the many conversations taking place around me.

There is a lot of love in this room, and it fuels a satisfying contentment.

I get home around eight. Daryl drops off Emily and Amber shortly after that, and I introduce Clark. After a curt "Hi," Amber takes off for her room, but Emily lingers downstairs. She starts asking questions about the ski trip we're taking the next day and shyly watches Clark.

He answers her questions and asks if she's going to be a ski bunny on the bunny slope. Emily gets silly and starts hopping around the room.

When she runs upstairs to fetch a toy she wants to show Clark—a stuffed bunny in a cute little dress—I smile.

Emily seems to like Clark already. The ski trip should be great.

Thank you, God, for all the wonderful people in my life!

-18-

Bunny Hopping on the Bunny Slope

THE NEXT MORNING only one other person is waiting at the church for a ride to the ski area—a young single man I've never met named Bob who also had never skied before. We all hop into Clark's Buick.

The black night melts into a peach-colored dawn. The road is a silver thread in a white-and-ochre patchwork quilt. The world is a spectacular, technicolor moving picture, and I had never noticed it before.

Where have I been?

The rise and fall of Emily's excited chatter is a happy bubbling brook, and Clark's questions and teasing comments keep the flow going the whole three-hour trip.

The boots I rent at the ski shop are heavy, and I feel awkward but still willing to give skiing a try. Clark helps Emily with her boots, and we lug our skis out the door, clomping like space men.

The air is so fresh and the sky is so blue, I feel exhilarated. Clark shows Bob and me how to fall and get up again and how

71

to hold the tow rope to let it pull us to the top of the bunny slope. Then he explains a snowplow position and makes us practice it.

Bob and I practice all morning on the bunny slope while Emily zips down it like a pro—her father had taken her skiing the previous winter. Then Clark guides all four of us up the combination of lifts that will take us to the top of the mountain.

We eat lunch in a restaurant at the top—barbecued sausages and potato chips—and when we go back outside, I notice the sky has grown cloudy.

I am nervous.

I'd ridden up on the ski lifts, careful to remind myself about what Clark had told me that morning. *When you reach the end of the lift, put your feet together and just stand up.* But as each lift carried me further and further up the mountain and I watched the ground pass by underneath my dangling legs, I kept thinking, how am I ever going to make it all the way back down?

Now it's time to do just that.

Clark is patient and shows us how to traverse the hill by snowplowing from one side of the run to the other, the right side to the left, in a zig-zag pattern. Then he skis down the slope toward the left a little ways, pirouetting backward and forward and backward again. He is good! He motions for me to follow.

I put my feet into snowplow position, concentrating on not letting the tips of my skis touch. As I ski closer, he shouts, "Now just point your skis toward me!" I do, but I am concentrating so hard, I forget how to stop. I crash into Clark, and we both end up in a heap on the snow.

He laughs and so do I, but I worry, too, that he will be embarrassed and won't want to take me skiing again. Maybe he won't even want to be seen with me. We must look very foolish, lying on the ground, entwined in a tangle of arms and legs.

Then he kisses me.

My eyes fly wide open. He stops suddenly and looks into my eyes. Then he puts one gloved hand behind my head, closes his eyes, and kisses me again. His lips are soft and warm.

Something inside my chest feels like a runaway snowball turning into an avalanche.

The snowball avalanche in my chest sprouts wings and takes off. Like an airplane, it angles up and rises above the clouds, right over the top of Keystone Mountain.

A few days later, my heart is still flying above Keystone Mountain when I get a card in the mail. I open its lavender envelope, recognizing the writing on the front as Clark's and read the words written inside:

> *If it can, it will be. If you are, then it must be. With God, it will always be. 932.8, Clark.*

Nine thirty-two point eight?

Yes! Now I remember! It's the code from our marathon phone conversation. I admitted to him that I set up barriers, that I hesitated to become romantically involved with anyone again, and that I would have a hard time saying "I love you" to anyone.

Clark responded by telling me something he learned in his communications class.

"'I love you' is only a bunch of words—a code," he said. "A person can call 'love' anything. As long as the meaning is clear to the receiver of the message, the code doesn't matter. For example, you could say something like, 'Nine thirty-two point eight,' and if we had agreed those words stood for love, it wouldn't matter. The meaning would be clear."

> *932.8, Clark.*

Love, Clark.

I feel my eyes grow watery, and then I look at the printed verse inside the card.

> *I have given myself to you and told you things that I've never told another soul.*

> *You are the one person who has seen me trembling and as fearful as an injured bird.*

> *You are the one person I always want to take with me when I feel exhilarated and my spirits are*

73

soaring.

I trust you with my secrets, and you now know that you can trust me with yours.

I have to put the card down. I can't see it anymore. I am overcome with emotion. And happiness.

And nine thirty-two point eight.

It was a perfect love story—as perfect as any human love story could ever be. We met in August and were married in December, just four months later. Every day after that ski trip was a dream come true. It was destined to go down in history as one of the greatest love stories and happy endings of all time.

I thought.

Dear God, thank you, thank you, thank you.

-19-

He Married Me for My Ankles

◻◇●◇◻

I PICK UP THE LIST and read it again, marking off the items one by one.

Buy sheet music—check.

Buy dress—check.

Make hair appointment—check.

Buy dresses for Amber and Emily—

Emily was eager to pick out a new dress for the wedding, and the one she selected was dark-red velvet with a broad, white lace collar. With her short blond hair, she looks like an angel in it.

Emily is thrilled, both about the wedding and about Clark. Whenever he comes over, she runs to him and throws her arms around his waist. Clark tickles her under her arms; sometimes that's the only way she will let go of her tight hold. She begs to be carried piggyback on his shoulders. She screams with excitement as he hoists her onto his back.

Sometimes I'm afraid she'll make a nuisance out of herself, and more than once I tell her, "Clark is not your own personal jungle gym!" But he's just a kid at heart himself, and I can tell he enjoys her spontaneity.

One night, Emily says that Clark is "Daddy," and her real father is "Dad." I'm grateful she's accepted Clark into her life so easily.

Amber is less enthusiastic, and I figure it might be a little more difficult for her to adjust to having a stepfather. It's hard to tell. Her sweet and flexible childhood personality, after turning fifteen, transformed into that of a typical uncommunicative teenager.

But she seems to like Clark. I overheard her laughing at some absurd statement he made last night while they were having a long conversation about teenage boys in general and Marty, in particular.

I wonder again if I am letting her get too involved with Marty too soon, but I know that if I say anything, she will call me a hypocrite. I sigh and return to my list.

Make appointment for counseling—

Clark and I went to the first session of our premarital counseling last week, and tomorrow is the next appointment. Gail, the assistant pastor and director of the Single's Program at our church, agreed to perform the ceremony and strongly urged us to take counseling. We took personality tests the previous week and will learn the results tomorrow, but I'm not worried.

I already know in my heart that we are right for each other.

I know Clark isn't perfect. I know that he's inclined to be impatient and intense, to try too hard. When he tries to do the opposite—to appear nonchalant by making jokes and smart remarks—people sometimes think he's callous or shallow. I know it's just a cover.

At the counseling session the next day, Gail explains the results of our personality tests.

"Now I don't want you to think that this is some sort of foolproof test of whether your marriage will be successful," she begins. "This test was designed to indicate any potential problem areas you, as a couple, might experience. The statistics say that three-out-of-four second marriages will fail. But if a couple is aware of potential problems before they occur, it can help them to resolve any differences they might have."

She holds up two charts. They look like erratic Dow Jones averages in a confused economic climate. But the pattern of each is similar, so similar that some of the dots are in the same spot on both charts.

"Susan, you're an INFJ and Clark, you're an INTP," she explains. "Your results are similar, but there's one area of variance where you might find potential discord. Susan, you prefer a more predictable lifestyle than Clark. You are probably the type of person who feels more secure planning things in advance, making lists..."

As she continues, I try not to giggle. Lists are my life.

The day of the wedding quickly arrives. We didn't invite many people, just family and close friends from church and from work. Jim takes pictures.

Clark and I slowly march to the front of the church, arm-in-arm behind Russ and Amber, then Emily and Bill, just like we practiced.

I look into Clark's eyes as the musician plays the first song, "The Rose." Clark looks at me and his eyes are getting red and watery. He tries to keep the tears from seeping out.

Then he takes my hand, mouths the words, "I love you," and Gail begins the ceremony.

We'd decided to postpone taking a real honeymoon until we had more time and money, but Russ hands us forty dollars to go out to dinner. We have steak and champagne and hold hands under the table.

I tell Clark about the first time I saw him and how I wanted to talk to him after the class was over but had been too shy to think of anything to say.

Clark tells me about the first time he noticed me in the class. He says he kept staring at my ankles wondering if I would go out with him.

"Your ankles. That's what I first noticed about you."

"My ankles? What's wrong with them?"

"Nothing. That's just it. They're so nice and slender. They have a nice shape. They're the most perfect ankles I've ever seen."

77

"I can't believe this. You married me for my ankles!"

"Yes. But lucky for me, everything else comes with them," Clark said with a smile.

Wanda is keeping the girls overnight, and Clark and I go home to a dark apartment. As we approach the door, Clark's arm shoots out in front of me, stopping me from entering. Did he see a prowler? Then he turns toward me and picks me up like a sleepy child.

"I have to carry you across the threshold, don't I?" he asks. "Isn't that how it's done?"

"What's done?" I laugh. "Getting a hernia?"

"Not at all. You're light as a feather."

But my feet stick out further than he anticipates, and he has to angle himself into the doorway. We're both laughing as he carries me up the stairs. When we get to the bedroom, he drops me on the bed.

We stay there for a long time.

Dear God, please let this happiness never end.

-20-

Curly, Dimpled Lunatics

□◇●◇□

"A child is a curly, dimpled lunatic."– Ralph Waldo Emerson

I T'S BEEN NEARLY a month since the wedding, and every day has been lovely—like Christmas Day—with a gift to unwrap.

This evening I'm reviewing Emily's math homework with her. She keeps saying she doesn't understand, but when I ask specific questions, she has a good grasp of the concepts.

Then, without warning, she bursts into tears.

"What's wrong, honey?"

I stroke her head and wait for the tears to subside.

"My teacher doesn't like me! I'm afraid I'm going to flunk!" she sobs.

"Oh honey. I'm sure she likes you. You are so lovable, how could she not?" I'm rewarded with a small smile.

Then I start wondering if the divorce caused some insecurities that are only now starting to show up.

Then again, maybe it really IS the teacher. Both Amber and Emily have a sixth sense when it comes to detecting other people's negative opinions. And they're both sensitive to criticism. I need to check this teacher out. Maybe her teaching style is too harsh.

While I'm helping Emily, Amber stalks around the room like a caged cougar.

"What's with you tonight?" Clark asks her. "You're not holed up in your room. What's the special occasion? Why are you gracing us with your presence?"

She glares at him, but he just gives her a harmless grin.

She seems to consider her choices for a moment, then sits down and responds without rancor, "I'm waiting for Marty to call."

I'm surprised. If I said what Clark just said, she would bite my head off. Hearing the words from Clark—with only humor in his voice—seems to make a difference.

"He's backed out of our date to go skating twice now. He said he'd call me tonight and let me know if he can go this Saturday."

"Ice or roller?" Clark asks.

"Ice."

"Has he ever been ice skating before?"

"No."

"Does he know you won trophies in ice skating?"

"Yeah, I showed them to him."

I can see where Clark's questioning is leading.

"Maybe he's making excuses because he can't skate."

"But I promised to teach him how to skate."

"Boys don't like to feel they aren't as good as a girl at doing something," he tells her. "It messes up their egos. Especially teenage boys."

The phone rings, and Amber flies down the hall to answer it. Emily, not wanting to be left out of the conversation, goes over to the rocking chair Clark is sitting in, climbs on his lap and wraps her arms around his neck. "Daddy, will you take me skating sometime?"

"Ice or roller?"

She thinks for a moment. "Have you ever ice skated before?"

"Nope."

"Roller!" she says decisively. "Say yes. Please! Please!"

He grins at me and says to her, "Your mom likes to ice skate. I think we should go ice skating."

Amber comes back into the living room. "He's going," she announces.

She takes Clark's hand and pulls him up from the chair. "You have to help me decide what to wear." Emily is still clinging to his neck.

"Emily!" Amber says. "Let go! Clark needs to help me decide what to wear."

Clark unwraps Emily's arms from around his neck. Her eyes get red and her mouth droops, but her about-to-fall teardrops dry up when he lifts her onto his shoulders. With Emily perched on his back like a monkey, he follows Amber upstairs to play the requested part of fashion consultant.

We all go ice skating that Saturday—Marty, too. Clark gamely rents skates and wobbles his way around the rink a few times on his own. I'm much better on ice skates than skis, and it's my turn to skate backward, watching and encouraging him.

He isn't bad. He doesn't have that stiff look of naked fear and helplessness most beginning ice skaters do.

After fifteen or twenty minutes he is confident enough to experiment with the mechanics of turning around to skate backward. I turn around and skate forward, pushing him slowly with my hands against his chest. He puts his arms out straight ahead and rests them on my shoulders.

"Look at Marty and Amber," he says.

I look. Amber, holding both of Marty's hands in hers, is trying to coax him away from the edge of the rink. He is smiling but looks very nervous.

"I don't think Marty's having a good time," Clark says. "Did Amber tell you what Marty said about our wedding?"

'No, what?" I ask.

"He told her that when he gets married, he wants her to wear a long dress instead of a short one like you did."

"What is he talking about? He can't be serious. He's only sixteen and Amber's only fifteen. She's... Give me a break! He didn't really say that did he?"

"You still think of Amber as your baby. She doesn't think she's a child anymore and Marty doesn't either."

"Well, they're both wrong."

"She's only got a little over two years left before she's out of high school. How old were you when you got married?"

"You know how old. Eighteen. But that wasn't one of my smarter moves. Amber's got more sense than that—at least I hope she does."

"She's got a bad case of 'Marty,' he responds.

I feel a shove from behind and arms around my waist. Emily is pushing me and giggling.

"You're not pushing fast enough! Daddy wants to go faster!"

"'Daddy's going fast enough," Clark tells her. With a grin, he reaches behind me to try and grab her shoulder, but he trips me with his skate.

I lose my balance and fall sideways, knocking Clark over. Laughing, Emily trips, too, and falls down on top of both of us.

The following evening, Emily brings up the topic of her bed, an item that's been high on her list of wishes for her ninth birthday. Although she's been saving money for a waterbed, she doesn't have quite enough. She also knows that getting it set up in her bedroom is beyond her capabilities, so she's asked us to help her as a birthday present.

"I can pay for almost all of it," she says. "There's just a little bit of help I need. I can show them where to set it up, and I can help set it up, and I can put water in it with my bucket."

Clark laughs. "I don't think your bucket will cut it, Squirt. Seems to me that you'll need a lot of help, not just a little."

Emily's lower lip juts out. "That's not so! I can be lots of help."

"So that's all you want for your birthday?" I ask, but the phone rings and cuts off her response.

"Susan? This is Maggie McCabe, Marty's mother."

I'd never spoken with her before, but I can discern tension in her voice.

"Amber is here with Marty, and she says she won't come home."

"What are you talking about?" I ask with rising concern.

"Amber is very upset. She says she needs some time to think about her future."

"What are you talking about?" I say more loudly. "Please put her on the phone!"

I can feel Clark's eyes on me while I wait for Amber to answer.

But I don't hear Amber's voice. It's Mrs. McCabe again.

"Amber says she doesn't want to talk to you right now."

"What?! Why not?!"

"It's alright if she stays with us. I'm sure things will straighten themselves out."

I'm stunned into silence as she hangs up. I'm listening to a dial tone.

"What?" Clark says.

"I don't know what just happened!" I say as I sink into a chair.

I repeat the conversation to Clark. He asks questions but is as clueless as I am about Amber's odd behavior. Then I take note of Emily's worried eyes on me.

"Isn't Amber coming home?" she asks in a quivering voice.

I realize then that I can't fall apart in front of Emily, so I tell her, "She's just going to stay at Marty's house overnight. That's all."

But Emily is smart, and I'm not sure my simple explanation satisfactorily covers for my previously disturbed demeanor.

83

Clark catches on and says to her, "Show me again where this waterbed is going to go."

Emily grabs his hand and pulls him up the stairs, leaving me in a confused state, still wondering, as my mother would say, "what has gotten into" Amber.

Dear God, please help me connect better with my daughters.

-21-

Space Shuttles and Spaceships

□◇●◇□

TUESDAY, JANUARY 28TH, the space shuttle is scheduled for another flight. I'm excited to watch this launch because some of the modules I built and tested will be onboard.

Jim and I walk down to the break room around ten a.m. to find a place to sit among the group already gathered to watch while the NASA launch facility in Cape Canaveral, Florida prepares for the launch. Thirty minutes later, Space Shuttle Challenger takes off with a roar and seven astronauts as we all cheer and applaud.

About one minute after take-off, Space Shuttle Challenger appears to explode in a bright flash of fire and huge plumes of smoke.

Within seconds, a few pieces of the shuttle continue on in an upward trajectory surrounded by white smoke, then slowly change course and fall toward the earth. Then there is nothing. Silence fills the room, followed by shocked questions.

Within hours, we learn that what we had just witnessed was a tragedy of epic proportion to the Space Shuttle Program. Space Shuttle Challenger caught fire in mid-air and all seven astronauts are presumed dead. [4]

I am horrified at the event I just witnessed and crushed when I think about the pain the families must be feeling. I also begin to worry—*What if something I did during my work on the modules caused the shuttle to explode?*

No one seems to know what might've caused the accident, and logically speaking, they might never know because the damage appears to be extensive. However, I silently worry.

□◇●◇□

That evening I finally have a chance to talk to Amber on the phone for a brief time, but I still can't get her to agree to meet with us or even talk about her reason for wanting to live at Marty's house.

Now it's Wednesday evening, and Clark and I have come up with a plan. Amber isn't going to like it, but I don't know of a better alternative. My tension is high, and I can't sit still.

The dispatcher at the police station is very nice after I explain my dilemma and says she believes I'm taking the right course of action. She tells me that Amber will be classified as a "runaway" and an officer will pick her up and drive her to our apartment within the hour.

Forty minutes later, the doorbell rings. I open the door and get only a glimpse of a red-faced angry Amber as she flies past me and runs up the stairs. I turn to the officer and thank him. He is very kind and seems sympathetic to my plight.

The second stage of our plan is now going into effect. I take a deep breath and head up the stairs to break the news to Amber that she will not be allowed to see Marty except in school and that she will be living with Wanda until we are all comfortable with her living at home again. She will also be going to counseling sessions with a psychologist that our pastor told us was particularly good with teens and young adults.

Not long after our conversation, Wanda arrives as preplanned to pick up Amber. I sit down and breathe a sigh of relief.

The plan is working so far, but what now? How do we get past this and return to some semblance of normalcy?

□◇●◇□

A few days later, unable to contain her excitement, Emily is jumping up and down like a whack-a-mole while she waits for

86

her dad to pick her up for the birthday party he and his new wife Pam have planned.

I'm unsure whether she's excited for her birthday party or for the new waterbed sitting in a box in the living room waiting to be hauled upstairs and assembled. Or maybe it's both.

A horn honks, and Emily races out the door with a quick good-bye kiss and hug for Clark and me.

Clark struggles a little as he picks up the box containing the waterbed parts.

"Do you need help with that?" I ask.

He manages to stand upright and shakes his head as he walks toward the stairs. I follow behind, figuring I can at least break his fall if he slips on the stairs.

Three hours later, he takes the hose out of the waterbed and tightens the cap. He then sits on the narrow edge of the wooden waterbed frame, collapsing backward because it's too small to balance on, capturing my hand as he falls.

We fall into a heap on the bed, bouncing a few times. I smile at him. Emily will be thrilled.

◻◇●◇◻

Emily's ninth birthday, Saturday February 8, 1986. A date that began the most eventful year of my life.

I know I made mistakes. But that's just what they were—mistakes—not intentional harm or even neglect. They were the kinds of mistakes millions of parents make with their children every day because parents are imperfect humans unable to predict the future.

Our disaster had an innocuous beginning, much like the simple mistake of not fully understanding the effects of cold temperature on the Challenger's "O" ring seal. Investigators had determined that the seal failed during liftoff and allowed hot gas to leak and ignite the fuel tank. The Challenger disaster was not caused by something I did.

But just four days after Emily's birthday, February 12, 1986, an alien spaceship crashed into our little family, smashed it into a thousand pieces, and dropped the leftover pieces of us on another planet. I spent an entire year longing to go back to my dear planet Earth where things made sense.

On this alien planet nothing made sense, and pain lurked around every corner. It knocked me down when I least expected it. Up was down, left was right, white was black. Good was bad, and bad was good. Truth was called a lie, and lies were told without repercussion. The alien planet was spinning and left me with nothing steady to hold on to.

There are people who would say, "It could've been worse," but they are viewing this from a future perspective. I agree, it could've *ended* worse, but from my perspective at the time, we were barreling full speed toward the worst possible ending. So, for me, it was already pretty bad.

All I can do is tell my story and describe how the events affected me. There are no words in the dictionary to adequately portray the emotional extremes I endured that year, and my description will, without a doubt, be inadequate.

But I will give it a shot.

Dear God, please guide me through this valley in the shadow of death.

□◇●◇□

Future Shock

Jesus come and set me free
from seeds of doubt when I foresee
my future in hyperbole
I need to know you're here with me

-22-

Dropped on Another Planet

◻◇●◇◻

I WAS RIGHT. Emily is thrilled with the waterbed. She bounces around the room like a ping pong ball in a room full of mouse traps. But she doesn't want to sleep on it in the normal way. She drags out her sleeping bag, a mummy-style bag, and carefully lays it on top of the bedspread.

"Why do you want to sleep in your sleeping bag, Emily?" Clark asks her when he sees the arrangement. "I thought you wanted a waterbed. I guess we should take it back since you prefer the sleeping bag."

Emily, not hearing the teasing tone in his voice, abruptly says, "No! You can't take it back! I love my waterbed. I'm just getting my sleeping bag into practice for the slumber party." She is referring to a classmate's sleepover that will take place next weekend. It seems that she plans to sleep in the sleeping bag on top of the waterbed all week.

Her dad had dropped her off earlier that day so we could have a small birthday party for her. Amber is still staying with Wanda, so it's just the three of us. After dinner and two helpings of cake and ice cream each, I bring up a subject with Emily that I'd been thinking about for the past couple of days.

"Emily, I know you mentioned that you don't think your teacher likes you. Have you thought about talking with her about it?"

89

She looks alarmed. "NO! I couldn't do that. She's too scary."

"It might be the best way to resolve the problem, Emily. I think she does like you, but she needs to know you think that. How else will she be able to tell you that she *does* like you if she doesn't know that you think she doesn't?"

I know it sounds a little convoluted, but I'm hoping Emily will understand what I am trying to say. I'm thinking that if the teacher knows how she comes across to students like Emily, maybe she will soften her manner a little.

The following afternoon, Emily skips happily up the stairs. She says, "I did it Mom! I talked to Mrs. Cann! She said she was glad I told her."

"That's great, Emily! What did she say?"

"Can I have some cookies and milk?" she responds. Food is uppermost in her mind.

While Emily sits at the table dunking her cookies into the milk, I try again. "What did Mrs. Cann say when you told her you thought she didn't like you?"

Emily shrugs. "I guess that I was wrong. Then she asked a bunch of questions."

"What kind of questions?" A knot is beginning to form in the pit of my stomach, although I can't say for sure why.

"Oh, just stuff. Like what is going on at home. I told her about getting a new daddy."

"Was that it?" I ask.

"Oh, and about Amber running away from home," She continues. "That was all."

I'm not liking the sound of this. It sounds as if the teacher thinks Emily's problem is something going on at home and isn't taking any responsibility for Emily's feelings. I decide to call the school the next day and make an appointment to talk to Mrs. Cann.

The next day, I make an appointment for the following Monday since that's my day off. I feel better having taken that step, but I am still a little disquieted.

I never made it to that appointment, however, because four days later, aliens landed in the middle of our home and ripped our lives apart.

□◇●◇□

I don't remember driving home from the DSS building after the social worker told me that Clark had molested Emily, but I must've made it without incident. Shortly after I arrived, Clark walked in the door, home from his shift at UCCS.

He could tell I was shaken. "What's wrong?" he asked.

I didn't know what to say. How do you tell your brand-new wonderful husband— whom you are madly in love with—that he has been accused of molesting your daughter?

I covered my face. I was openly crying. Clark sat down in front of me on the stairs, took my hands, and slowly lowered them.

"Are you going to tell me what's wrong or am I going to have to beat it out of you?"

His words had the intended effect. I chuckled a little, still sobbing, and told him what the social worker told me.

His face had turned to ash by the time I was done, and he said, "Why?? Why would Emily lie about me?"

"I'm not sure she did." I responded. My eyes were starting to burn from the salty tears. "I've been wondering if there is some kind of mistake. If they would just let me talk to Emily, maybe I could find out where this is coming from. I just can't picture Emily saying it though. She loves you. She wants to hang out with you all the time. She..."

I glanced back to his face and stopped talking. Tears were leaking from his eyes, and he tried to wipe them away before I saw them.

His voice was tight with stress. "I would never hurt Emily. You don't think I did this, do you?"

I searched his face. All I could see was pain and hurt. Nothing that would indicate concern over being "caught." I thought about his behavior. He hadn't shown any evidence of sexual attraction toward Emily or Amber or any other children. I

91

thought about our own sex life. It was honeymoon sex— fulfilling and frequent—and adult.

"No, I don't believe you are a child molester. Now we just have to get to the bottom of why that social worker thinks you are."

Dear God, please give me the strength I need to fight for my family.

-23-

Examined by Aliens

◻◇●◇◻

MEMO FOR THE RECORD written June 9, 1986, by Susan Gabriel:

On Feb 12, 1986, my younger daughter Emily (age 9) was removed from the school and placed into foster care by the Department of Social Services (DSS). I was contacted by the intake worker Paula Randall and told that my daughter had reported being sexually molested by my husband, Clark. She warned me that I must be totally supportive of Emily, believe that she had been molested and do everything the DSS required, or I might never have Emily returned to me. She mentioned that divorcing my husband would be best.

The following day I contacted our attorney, who had the temporary custody hearing date set back a week. A few days later I contacted Dr. Cherre Torok, the psychologist who was seeing Amber. After discussing the situation with both of them, we were advised not to move Clark out of the home, as that would be viewed as an admission of guilt.

This description was included in a Memo for Record my lawyer suggested I write to submit to Family Court. It's a short summary of the early details.

A few days after they took Emily, both Clark and I were separately interviewed by the DSS. Clark's interview lasted less than five minutes.

He was too angry to talk about what was said when he walked out of the interviewing room, but he later told me that the caseworker just laughed when he asked for something in writing that detailed what he was accused of doing.

When it was my turn, I left angry, too. My interview went something like this:

> **Caseworker:** *We know your husband is guilty. You've got to force him to admit it.*
>
> **Me:** *How do you know he's guilty?*
>
> **Caseworker:** *Because he says he's innocent. Guilty people always say they're innocent.*
>
> **Me:** *But what do innocent people say?*
>
> **Caseworker:** *We're not in the business of determining guilt or innocence. We're in the business of putting families back together again.*
>
> **Me:** *Then why not do that with us?*
>
> **Caseworker:** *Because Clark won't admit his guilt.*

Clark was also interviewed on February 19th by Detective Teasdale from the Colorado Springs Police Department. Clark knew he was innocent, so he saw this as a way to get the misunderstanding cleared up quickly.

When speaking with the detective, he agreed to take a polygraph—a "lie detector test." He thought this would clear him of the allegation.

We found out later from our attorney that, ironically, the police are allowed to lie about lie detector results since they aren't admissible in court because of their inherent unreliability.

The police invited Clark to go down to the station to "discuss" the results—in reality, they were planning to coerce Clark into admitting guilt to the alleged "crime."

When they told him that he'd lied, Clark asked, "What about?"

When they said "Everything," Clark sarcastically asked, "Even my name?"

When he realized he couldn't have a rational conversation with them, he told them there was no point in discussing it, and he left.

With each discussion or interview Clark had with someone from the child protection system, his steadfast refusal to admit to a crime frustrated and infuriated them. As a result, they were even more determined to prosecute both of us and make sure Emily was never returned home—not because it was dangerous for her—but because they wanted to punish us for not bending to their will.

There is one question that everyone asks, and I will answer it now. That question is, "What started this ball rolling in the first place?"

It was several days before we found out ourselves. Our attorney petitioned the court for documents so we could see what initiated the investigation.

Finally, we found out. It turned out to be this—which I've copied from a summary my attorney suggested I write to submit to the court to "fill in the blanks" in their version of events:

> *The allegation of sexual abuse by my husband, Clark Gabriel, was based on information obtained by the Police Department's Youth and Victims Service (YVS) worker, Barbara Midyett, during an interview with my daughter on February 12, 1986, as a result of a conversation Emily had with her third-grade teacher, Mrs. Cann. The conversation was initiated by Emily at my suggestion after she reported to me she was afraid of the teacher and was having problems completing her homework.*

> *Mrs. Cann, rather than directly addressing Emily's problems with her teaching style, began questioning Emily about her home life, and specifically about her new stepfather, Clark. Emily reportedly stated that he had tickled her on the knee.*

After a consultation with her principal, Mrs. Cann called in a report of suspected abuse. The following day, Barbara Midyett and Dick Brown from YVS were dispatched to the school [accompanied by police] to interview Emily.

*Although the reported suspected abuse was based on knee tickling, Barbara Midyett [assumed a crime had occurred and] began her written report by stating, "Prior to Officer Gurule's arrival at the school **to take a report of incest...** "*

Ms. Midyett's report, which she admitted she wrote more than a week after the interview, contained information she allegedly obtained from Emily when no one else was present. The interview was not recorded on tape, and the notes she took during the interview were not available because she had destroyed them.

She further testified that she had interviewed me, and then she described my state of mind during the supposed interview. In reality, I never had an interview with Ms. Midyett and, in fact, to this day have never met her.

Barbara Midyett's supplemental report was written *after* we were interviewed by the DSS and refused to cooperate with them. Her report included a touching allegation against Clark that was more specific—that he touched her between the legs, but over her underwear one night.

Did she write the supplemental report because we weren't cooperating and they needed a stronger allegation? Or did she have us confused with another family whose child she had also interviewed?

Dear God, please help me to stand strong and do what's right.

-24-

Questions with No Answers

□◇●◇□

WE HAD MANY QUESTIONS.

For example, how can someone be charged with a crime based on an interview with a nine-year-old child where nothing was recorded, there were no witnesses to the conversation, and all notes were destroyed? This can't happen in the United States, can it? Aren't there protections in place? Isn't some kind of evidence of a crime needed?

These were the questions we kept asking, but no one gave us a satisfactory explanation.

I kept wondering if there was something I could've done to prevent what had happened, and I often felt depressed about it. I reviewed my own actions up, down, back, forth, inside out and outside in, right side up, and upside down. Then I did it again. And again.

I knew I made mistakes. For example, I might have gone to the school to talk to Emily's teacher first, before she had a chance to misconstrue Emily's distress and blame it on her home life. It might have been helpful to take Emily for counseling during the same time Amber was going to counseling, which was shortly before the DSS "kidnapped" Emily.

The mistakes I made were due to my human inability to predict the future.

The mistakes I made weren't the kind of mistakes that DSS wanted me to acknowledge, however. They believed my mistakes were (1) sticking up for Clark, (2) not believing everything they said, and (3) not going along with every recommendation they made.

After all, they had control of Emily for the foreseeable future. Didn't I want her back home with me? What kind of mother was I?

They used my love for Emily as a weapon against me.

The anguish I experienced at this point was so intense, at times it was unbearable. And when I imagined how Emily was feeling, it compounded the pain until I was sure it would drive me insane.

Added to the extreme anguish was sadness. I missed Emily tremendously. When she was a baby, I was never reluctant to get up at night to feed her. I held her in my arms long after her bottle was empty, just rocking and enjoying her soft presence.

I loved watching the joyful way she approached new adventures, and I longed to experience them with her again. She was my baby, and I just couldn't get used to the idea of losing her.

The first time I saw Emily after they took her was at the DSS building on February 20th. The preliminary hearing was scheduled for that day, also, but our attorney had the date moved out a week to give us time to better understand why the DSS took Emily.

When I got there, I was directed to a room where there were a few tables and chairs and a limited number of toys. I signed in at the desk, and they brought Emily in.

They had instructed me prior to the meeting that I was not allowed to talk with her about anything related to the reason she was taken by DSS.

It broke my heart when they brought Emily in. She was sad and obviously in distress. She wore a dirty dress that was several sizes too small for her.

Why hadn't they asked me to bring clothes for her? I could've brought some if the foster home didn't have any. I could tell she hadn't brushed her teeth or had her hair combed for at least a couple of days, maybe more. I resolved to bring what she needed to my next scheduled visit with her.

I took out my comb and gently worked through the knots in her hair while she sat in my lap and cried. I had tears in my eyes, too. And, of course, the first question she asked was, when would she get to come home? And the second question was, why couldn't she go home now?

Since they had warned me not to talk about that or they would cancel visitations altogether, I just held her and told her I loved her and I wasn't sure when she would be able to come home.

That evening, Emily called me on the phone from the foster home.

Crying softly at first, she told me about the confrontation she'd had with Paula Randall after Paula told her she couldn't go home.

"She was yelling at me and grabbing my shoulders and shaking me." Emily sobbed. "She was screaming, 'It's not my fault you can't go home, it's your mother's fault! She won't make your stepfather move out!'"

Emily was so upset, I had to listen carefully to understand what she was saying.

I told her that I loved her and wanted her home and that we didn't even get to talk to the judge because the date was set back. I said Clark was willing to move out, but other people told us he shouldn't.

At this point she burst out, "I don't understand! There are two stories here. Paula said it was your fault!"

The call ended abruptly as if someone had hung up the phone on her end. I was overcome with anger and shock. Paula Randall was purposely trying to destroy my relationship with Emily!

The following morning Emily called me again. She started the conversation with the words, "Mom, what if I lied?"

I assured her that I would still love her, but in the background I could hear an adult saying something about hanging up the phone. The conversation again ended abruptly.

I was anxious and alarmed. I hoped she didn't suffer abuse at the hands of the foster parents for breaking the rules. Every time I thought about Paula Randall shaking Emily and shouting, I stopped what I was doing and prayed for Emily. It was the only way I could calm my nerves and control my anger.

I was on edge all afternoon. Did she tell her foster parents the abuse didn't happen? Would the DSS realize they had made a mistake and let her come home?

That evening I received a call from Paula Randall, and she told me that Emily had been removed from foster care and placed with her father Daryl. She also said I would be allowed no more than two one-hour visits per week with Emily at my ex-husband's convenience and under his supervision to ensure I didn't break the rules "again."

She also said I was no longer allowed to speak with Emily on the phone because I "hadn't handled it very well."

I was devastated, angry, and discouraged.

Clark was arrested in March, a month after Emily was taken, and charged with one case of "sexual assault on a minor by a person in a position of trust." It carried a penalty of up to sixteen years in prison. It would have been eight years if Clark had been a stranger to Emily, but as her stepfather, that put him into the category "position of trust," which doubled the maximum sentence.

I was charged in Family Court with not sufficiently protecting Emily from the alleged abuse, which opened a Dependency and Neglect case in family court. I was required to go to court for hearings on various motions about once a month.

The burden of proof in family court—unlike in criminal court where it's "beyond a reasonable doubt"—is much lower. And the "evidence" presented could consist of merely a caseworker's testimony or written report without any accompanying proof of validity.

Everything provided by a professional child protection system (CPS) worker was accepted by the judge without question and given more weight than anything presented by us, our attorney, or our expert witnesses.

The deck was purposely stacked against us.

God, please help us hold on until we are rescued!

◻◇●◇◻

God's Reclamation Project

Flotsam submerged
Hope hit an iceberg
Who can salvage sad debris
sunk in misery?

-25-

The Professional Child Abusers

□◇●◇□

IN EARLY MARCH, we decided to bring Amber back from Wanda's house to live with us again.

We picked her up and brought her home, but the second she set foot in the door, she turned around and darted out. Always quick with his reflexes, Clark leaped off the front porch and ran after her, catching her around the waist just as she rounded the corner of the apartment building.

He picked her up while she kicked and screamed like a wildcat. Clark never let go and carried her up the stairs, with me trailing close behind. He tossed her on our bed, and I shut the bedroom door.

He sat down next to Amber and said, "What do you think of the situation with Emily?"

Amber said nothing.

Clark asked, "Can you explain your behavior? Why did you run away to live at Marty's house?"

Amber said she didn't want to talk about it.

"Ok, then, you can just sit and listen to your mother and me."

Clark asked me how I was doing, then asked me to go into detail about what had been happening with Emily. I repeated all the events, talking about how frightened I was and how devastated I felt. At one point, Amber started to say something, and Clark said to her, "No, you said you didn't want to talk. You will just listen."

A few minutes later, Amber started to cry. She sobbed that she was sorry she had been so difficult. I cried, too, and I think Clark also shed a few tears. That event cleared the air, and her behavior improved after that. She was supportive and loving again—to the extent a fifteen-year-old can be.

I later asked Amber why she ran away to Marty's house. She said she'd been disappointed that I got remarried, and she was afraid a new stepfather would treat her the same way her father had. Over the next few months, however, she saw that Clark wasn't anything like Daryl, and their relationship continued to improve.

Although Emily was now living with Daryl and his new family, our relationship with her was completed controlled by others.

It was obvious that Daryl and Pam bought into the idea of Clark as a pedophile, and they took their task of following DSS's rules seriously.

Amber was able to visit Emily on weekends at their father's house, but Daryl or Pam monitored everything. Amber never stayed long because she found it nerve-wracking to be constantly watched.

I could only see Emily at Daryl's house or the DSS facility and only under supervision to make sure we didn't break the rules.

I was limited to two visits a week with Emily—one hour per visit—and only when it was convenient for Daryl and Pam. Conversation was severely restricted.

I became very anxious about going to their house and enduring their judgmental expressions. Before the first month was up, I asked to have all the visits with Emily scheduled at the DSS facility again.

Emily wasn't allowed to see Clark at all, and she missed him.

No phone calls were allowed.

Nothing about our relationship was normal.

Emily was being held for "ransom" until I did what the DSS wanted me to do — kick Clark to the curb and cooperate in his prosecution. My heart broke over and over again. It was torture, a never-ending nightmare.

Several times people asked me, "Why didn't you just do what they said so you could get Emily back?"

I questioned myself and doubted myself and fought with myself over and over until I finally reached a logical and permanent decision about it.

There were three main reasons:

(1) If I cooperated with them, I would be helping to convict an innocent man of a crime and ruining his life. It was wrong, and my conscience would kill me.

(2) After Emily grew up and realized the role she had played in the conviction of an innocent man, she would likely experience intense guilt for her involvement in ruining his life. I didn't want her to go through that.

(3) I would not be a good role model if I caved to outside pressures. A person needs to stay strong and stand up for what's right—that's the message I wanted to send to both my daughters.

But it was killing me to see what anguish Emily was going through because she was denied a normal family life with us. The pressure on me to cave was intense, and I started seeing a psychiatrist. He prescribed a medication for anxiety called Xanax.

It made me feel weird and tired, so I didn't take it regularly. I only took it when I was particularly anxious.

This wasn't the way it was supposed to be taken.

I went to therapy sessions with the psychiatrist for a few weeks, but I stopped going and changed therapists when he asked me these questions, "Why can't you just get over this? What is keeping you from moving forward?"

I was appalled at his callousness. Of course, I couldn't move forward—did he not understand that our family was being tortured and extorted? My husband had been charged with a felony he didn't commit, trials for both of us were looming, and my daughter was being held for ransom!

I left that session and never went back. I read in our local newspaper a month later that the psychiatrist had been arrested for insurance fraud.

I guess helping people wasn't his primary motive, so it was just as well that I stopped going. I wouldn't have been able to continue seeing him anyway, what with his being in jail and all.

□◇●◇□

I found it ironic that the "child savers" couldn't see what was happening, that they were the ones inflicting pain, confusion, emotional injury, and psychological scars on our family. The need we had for counseling was due to their interference in our lives.

The court-appointed psychologist's reports about Emily described how traumatized she was, but they attributed it to having been abused by Clark. Yes, she *was* abused, I wanted to shout, but NOT BY US! *You* people committed the abuse and ought to be the ones on trial!

We were severely handicapped because we didn't understand how the Child Protection System worked at the time. We were clueless, ignorant, stumbling, bumbling children in a field filled with a cynical, battle-hardened alien attack force.

We had no idea that the child protection laws had been rewritten a few years before and normal constitutional protections eliminated.

We had no idea of the dangers that lurked around every corner.

I began to fear that God had abandoned us.

□◇●◇□

Prayer for Peace

Father God, please hear my plea.
I am here on bended knee.
Give me peace please, where there's none.
Father help me—fear has won!

-26-

And Then I Died—or So I Thought

◻◇●◇◻

DARYL HAD THREE stepsons from his new marriage with Pam—he finally got the boys he wanted.

Although he and I had joint custody of the girls before they took Emily, they lived with me the majority of the time. And since he was busy with three stepsons, that worked out well for all of us.

Until now, it seemed.

In June—four months after they took Emily—Daryl petitioned the court to give him full custody of her and to allow him to stop making all child support payments. This would terminate my custody rights.

I was furious when I read his petition and the way it was phrased. It was obvious that he would be joining with the CPS to prosecute both Clark and me:

A Dependency and Neglect action is presently pending in the court regarding this matter... Petitioner believes that Emily would be in grave physical danger and her emotional development would be significantly impaired if she were allowed to return to the

106

care, custody, and control of the respondent....Petitioner respectfully moves this court for an order awarding the care, custody, and control of the minor child, Emily L. Dickinson to the petitioner and restricting any visitation with respondent to specifically exclude the respondent's husband Clark Gabriel, from the visitation and require that the visitation be supervised by the DSS.

It was one more nail in the coffin that trapped us.

◻◇●◇◻

The day of the hearing has finally arrived. Today I will find out the fate of my custody rights. I still have a shred of hope that the judge will rule in my favor and not end my joint custody.

I hope the Xanax I took kicks in soon. I need to keep my emotions in check no matter which way this goes.

I'm on pins and needles waiting for the judge to call our case file number. Finally, he calls it, and the judge makes his ruling.

Daryl is given full custody.

And I am given—

- No custody rights

- No more child support, even though Amber is still living with me

- Bi-weekly one-hour supervised visitations at DSS to be scheduled at Daryl's convenience

When I see Daryl's smirk, I really lose it. All I feel is white hot rage over what the system and my ex-husband are doing to us—taking Emily away, crushing her spirit, destroying her innocence—charging Clark with a felony—charging me with neglect—creating a never-ending churn of court hearings and making our lives a nightmare.

All I want is to be left alone to live in peace with my daughters and my new husband.

Anger flows through my veins and arteries until I am moving on fury-fueled automatic pilot, not really planning, just acting.

The next thing I know, I'm driving along a winding dirt road, wiping at the tears that continue to leak from my eyes and threaten to obscure my vision.

Once more I glance at the bag on the passenger seat that holds my future. Or rather, lack of one. Contents: everything with a warning label that I could grab before I changed my mind—one wine cooler, half a dozen pain pills, and two dozen Xanax tablets.

As the road grows narrower, pine and cedar branches brush against the car. I drive slower. Little more than a path, the surface's rocks and ruts make for a bumpy ride.

I look for familiar landmarks—the bent tree next to a large boulder, then the steep curve to the left before widening onto a small open space barely large enough to park two cars. Jim called it Brush Hollow.

I see the large flat rock. The last time I was here, I ate a picnic lunch on that rock with Jim. That was almost a year ago. Now I'm here again, and although I brought a lunch bag, I didn't bring a picnic.

Sobbing openly now, I grab my bag, open the car door, and slowly climb onto the rock. The rock's surface is warmed by the sun streaming down from a cloudless blue sky. I blink tears from my eyes as I look around at the trees surrounding the small clearing and sniff the cedar in the air. It's a good spot for dying.

I look at the pills in my hand.

Can I really do this? Dear Lord, what else can I do? I have totally and completely messed up the lives of the three people I love most in this world. Emily, Amber, Clark, I am so sorry! I know you'll be better off after I'm gone. And I will be better off without this searing pain that's ripping me apart and tearing holes in my soul!!

God, if you really exist, you'll have to do something if you want me to live. I can't try any more. I can't face it anymore. I just can't do it.

With that, I swallow the pills, a few at a time, with the help of the wine cooler. Then I lay down on the rock to die.

▫◇●◇▫

I lower myself to the curb in front of the grocery store. I don't know what I'm supposed to do now. I need to just sit here and think. I'll just sit here until I figure it out. A couple stares at me as they walk into the grocery store.

▫◇●◇▫

The man turns the paper around and points to the line where I'm supposed to sign my name.

I sign, and he tells me, "This is only for three days. After that, you'll be evaluated by the staff doctor to see if you can be released or need to stay with us a little longer."

A nurse leads me down a hallway that smells like pine cleaner and an unappetizing mixture of peas and fish. A high-pitched woman's voice floats out from a room as we pass by, "Help me! Help! You there! Come here!"

The nurse leads me to a small room with a bed, then tells me that she needs to take my shoes. She said she also needs to go through my bag. She removes two pens and a nail file and says they'll hold onto these until I am discharged.

My mind is so very fuzzy. I lie down on the bed and immediately drift into a restless sleep where giant talking rocks glare at me and tell me they are going to roll on top of Emily, Amber, Clark, and me and grind us into dust.

▫◇●◇▫

May cause reckless behavior, delirium, and increased thoughts of suicide.

Those are possible side effects of Xanax. Whether my emotional breakdown was the result of the Xanax, the stress or—more likely—a combination of the two, I can't say for sure. But I won't ever take that medication again.

I recounted only the parts of this event that I remember. So you're probably wondering, what happened exactly? How did I get from the flat rock to the grocery store to the hospital?

God, I'm alive. Why?

-27-

The Rest of the Story

◻◇●◇◻

HERE'S WHAT I KNOW, but only because I was told about it later. Even though I must've been partly conscious for those two days, I still don't remember anything except the small bit I described.

I vomited up the mixture of pills and alcohol, which I'd taken on an empty stomach. Then I drove several miles to Jim's house, where I showed up on his doorstep.

Here's what Jim told me about that day and the following day:

I don't remember the day or the time. It wasn't late, but it was dark out. The doorbell rang, and when I answered the door there you stood. You were wearing a white outfit that was a mess, as was the rest of you. All you said was, 'Can you help me? Something is biting me,' and you were feeling the back of your head.

A quick look showed the 'biting' thing was a piece of Cholla cactus. I got you to the sofa next to the light on the end table, and with the assistance of a pair of needle nose pliers and some scissors, managed to remove two pieces of cactus and a bunch of spines.

You told me you had tried to kill yourself with pills and a wine cooler but must have thrown up. Judging

110

from the red stains on your clothes I would agree with that. There were also grass stains, so you either rolled down a hill or fell at some point.

You were only semi-coherent and kept dozing off, so I didn't get a lot of information other than that you had been at Brush Hollow. I still don't know how you managed to find my house, let alone drive in that condition.

I checked your vital signs a couple of times, and every-thing seemed okay. I got you a damp cloth to clean up a little and convinced you to give me your skirt and jacket to wash while you took a nap.

After that, I convinced you to leave your car at my house and I took you home. When I dropped you off, Clark and Amber were still up. I told Clark I would let you explain what had happened.

The next day I got a call from you while I was at work. You were upset because the pharmacist wouldn't refill your prescription for more pills. You were still slurring your speech so I can see why he wouldn't. You kept saying you wanted to die and were going to find more pills. I finally got you to tell me where you were, and I went and picked you up at the store and took you home again.

I'd walked to the grocery store, which was about a mile from our house. Clark, who had gone to work to unlock the door so his staff could get in, returned home just as Jim arrived with me, then Clark drove me to the hospital, and well... now you're all caught up.

During my three-day stay in the hospital's psychiatric wing, I had to participate in group therapy and also one-on-one coun-seling sessions.

On my third day there, the psychiatrist assigned to my case said, "Well, I'm going to discharge you before this place makes you crazy." I laughed out loud.

I went back to work the next day. The only person at work who knew the truth about where I'd been was Jim, and he wasn't telling.

▫◇●◇▫

One day, a very kind man, one of the elders from our church, stopped by to see me. He asked me what had happened, and I told him the whole story.

Afterwards he said, "You don't have any emotional expression on your face when you talk about this. Your expression is very flat. Why is that?"

I didn't know what my face looked like. Did I feel flat? Yes, to some extent, I did. My emotions had been so overwhelmed for so long, I wasn't sure I had any left.

He prayed with me. Then he said, "Will you promise me something? The next time you feel like harming yourself will you call me first? I'm not asking you to do or not do anything, other than this. Just call me first. Will you do that?"

He was so kind, I couldn't let him down by refusing that one small request, so I agreed.

▫◇●◇▫

After I got home from the hospital, I was appalled that I'd almost left Amber and Emily motherless. It disturbed me greatly for several months, and I suffered a lot of guilt.

I sincerely thanked God that He saved me, and I was grateful for His intervention. I'd driven several miles in an extremely impaired condition and—miraculously—didn't have an accident. It was frightening that I didn't remember driving. It would have been disastrous if I'd injured or killed someone while driving in such an impaired condition.

I was also horrified that I'd dragged Jim into my suicide attempt after knowing that his wife had committed suicide. I later apologized for being so insensitive, and he said, "That's okay, I knew you weren't in your right mind."

The system kept grinding us down every day, though, and I eventually reached a point where I started to doubt that God even existed.

Dear God, are you there?

▫◇●◇▫

Dissolution

Tissue paper heart dissolves
and clings like a drowning victim
to a shape that used to look like hope

-28-

The Wheels Grind

◻◇●◇◻

BEFORE CLARK WENT to trial, the District Attorney's office, finally realizing how weak their case was against Clark, offered him a plea bargain. The plea agreement was called a Deferred Prosecution, which meant, if Clark didn't commit a crime for a year, they would dismiss the charges. If he did commit a crime, they could charge him again and take him to trial.

Clark continued to maintain his innocence and rejected the plea bargain. In spite of the attorney's explanation of how it was almost a dismissal of the charges, Clark asked for his day in court to prove his innocence.

This attitude irked the judge, who ordered our attorney to give Clark's file to his former law partner to review. He said he wanted to make sure that Phil, Clark's defense attorney, was giving Clark the right advice.

The judge's former law partner reviewed the file, then wrote this letter.

Sep 8, 1986

Dear Phil:

I have reviewed the Clark Gabriel file and cannot recommend to him that he accept the deferred prosecution offered in this case. I realize that a deferred prosecution is rarely offered and that in many ways, it is the equivalent to a dismissal of the charges. Indeed, in most cases, I would strongly urge the defendant to accept such an offer.

The problem with this case is that it is quite clear that Gabriel is simply not guilty of these charges:

(1) The child initially did not make allegations of sexual abuse, even though directly questioned by a schoolteacher and later by police and social service workers.

(2) The allegation was made only after she was privately questioned by social service workers, a situation that I have seen before.

(3) The child has since admitted that she initially told the truth and was lying to social service workers when she alleged sexual abuse, admitting this to her foster mother, and on more than one occasion, admitting it to her mother.

(4) The response of social services has been, not to reassess the validity of the charges or their own interviewing techniques, but to limit the child's contact with her own mother.

(5) The psychologist who has evaluated the child has voiced doubts about the truth of the allegations.

(6) The psychologist who evaluated the defendant indicates that he does not fit an abuser profile and the psychologist doubts the charges against him.

(7) Social Services has placed the child in "incest therapy," the tendency of which is to reinforce the allegations.

This case fits a disturbing pattern in which child protection workers induce the child to make allegations not originally made, then resist the child's effort to recant, and ignore reports by qualified experts questioning the truth of the child's allegations.

115

This case should not be kept alive by deferred prosecution or otherwise. If it is not dismissed, I must reluctantly recommend that the defendant undergo the risks of trial.

If he prevails, I strongly recommend that he file suit against the DSS, the individual caseworkers involved, and if the case law permits, against the DA's office and the prosecutors involved. I suggest that you file the necessary notice forthwith to protect Mr. Gabriel's rights to file such a case.

So, after reading this letter, the judge dismissed the charges, right? Or the prosecutors realized how weak their case was and requested the case be withdrawn?

Nope, on both counts. In fact, the judge was even more irked and privately told Phil that he intended to "throw the book" at Clark if he was convicted—to give Clark the maximum sentence of 16 years in prison—one more threat for not bending to their will.

◻◇●◇◻

With much trepidation, two months later, we went to trial.

The trial began Tuesday November 11, 1986. Clark had wisely requested a jury trial since the judge had already displayed his own personal bias against Clark.

But jury selection in Clark's trial took an unusual turn when they ran out of potential jurors. "Seating" a jury with the typical jury pool was usually easy, but in Clark's trial, the one question everyone stumbled over was, "Do you believe that children always tell the truth about abuse?"

The prevailing attitude in the court system and also in the general population was that accused child molesters were scum. Note I said "accused" and not "convicted."

The widely held view at that time was that "children never lie about abuse," so obtaining a child abuse conviction was not difficult for prosecutors. But it did make finding an unbiased jury difficult, so the judge ordered the bailiff to go to other departments in the courthouse to find people and press them into jury service. To their surprise, people who went to the courthouse to pay a fine or renew their driver's license found themselves instead serving on a jury.

Finally, enough jurors were found, and they were able to complete jury selection at the end of the first day.

Dear God, please help Clark get a not-guilty verdict!

□◇●◇□

The View from Here

They say we "see"
more perfectly
in darkest night
without our sight.
In midst of plight,
we seek the light.
But I don't want just light of dawn.
It is truth to which I'm drawn.

-29-

All Rise

□◇●◇□

BY THE TIME the actual trial started, the allegation against Clark—that he touched Emily between the legs, but over her underwear one night—consisted of details fabricated by someone who was unfamiliar with our home and our possessions. Emily had, most likely, been persuaded by someone on the prosecution's side to tell that story. We planned to demonstrate in court that the story was false.

But getting to that place meant calling Emily to the witness stand and recreating the scene of the alleged "abuse." I worried it was going to be traumatic for her because she would have to lie to keep up the charade and please the prosecutors. It also meant putting me on the witness stand, where I would have to keep my cool while being questioned by the prosecutor.

The prosecution tried to prevent Emily from testifying, but we needed her there, and our attorney eventually persuaded the judge that it was required by law because "the accused has the right to face his accusers in court."

None of the witnesses were allowed to watch any part of the trial, so that meant I had to spend my days chewing my nails while sitting on the bench outside the courtroom. I did get to hear a little about what happened each evening, but we needed to minimize my knowledge of what was going on to

118

avoid a mistrial, so it was only general information—nothing specific.

I did hear one interesting tidbit, though. The prosecutor saw Wanda sitting in the courtroom audience and believed she was me—Clark's wife—so he insisted that she leave the courtroom. With Wanda's dark hair and dark eyes, she looked nothing like Clark's blonde-haired, blue-eyed wife, me. It was more evidence that the prosecution's team didn't really know anything about our family and hadn't bothered to learn who we were.

A few days into the trial, my turn came to testify. I was terrified but tried not to show it. My testimony was crucial to show that the fabricated story Emily told in court couldn't have happened.

The story was that Clark came into her room one night, sat on the edge of her bed, and without unzipping her sleeping bag, reached down and put his hands between her legs. If Emily owned a regular bed and a regular child's sleeping bag, this would be awkward, but theoretically possible.

But Emily had the new waterbed with nothing solid to sit on. The frame that held the waterbed bladder was about an inch wide. In addition, Emily's sleeping bag was a mummy style bag that had been used for camping during cold Colorado high country weather. Slipping a man's hand into the bag would have been difficult but sitting on an inch-wide surface while doing so was impossible.

I gave these details calmly and kept my cool. Then it was the prosecutor's turn. He would have to try and salvage his case by weakening my testimony.

He started with a few questions about the bed and the sleeping bag, but when that only made the situation worse for him, he tried another approach.

"Ms. Gabriel, do you believe you are a good mother?"

I said "Yes," not quite sure what he was getting at.

Then he asked, "Did you raise Emily to always tell the truth?"

I responded "Yes, but..."

He immediately cut me off and said, "That's all for this witness, your Honor."

I helplessly looked at Phil, Clark's attorney.

He immediately read the situation and said, "Redirect, your Honor." Then he got up and asked me what else I wanted to say.

I was so relieved.

"I taught her to tell the truth, but she's only nine years old. She's not old enough yet to truly understand what that means," I said.

Then I was dismissed and escorted back to the hall to sit on my bench and gnaw on my knuckles since all my fingernails were chewed off.

Later that evening I learned that, as a final act of throwing caution to the wind and going against the collective advice of pretty much every defense attorney everywhere, our attorney let Clark go on the witness stand and testify. I wish I could have seen the prosecutor's expression when he heard Clark called to the stand to testify. It usually seals the deal—in favor of the prosecution.

After both sides rested their cases, the jury left the courtroom to deliberate. The trial had taken three days. Would they have a verdict before the weekend, or would we have to be on pins and needles until Monday? Or Tuesday? Or longer?

The jury came back in less than a day.

But before I tell you the verdict, I want to tell you about my work, my emotional state, and my spiritual life during this time.

We had significant expenses from this drawn-out catastrophic event—fees for lawyers, psychological evaluations, psychotherapy sessions, expert witnesses, investigators, consultants—tens of thousands of dollars. We had to borrow money to pay for all of it, so I had to make sure I didn't lose my job. I was very careful to make sure court and other appointments didn't conflict with work duties. The only person at work who knew what was really going on was Jim.

Work was a place of refuge where I could forget my problems for a few hours, at least until I got home to find new "letter bombs" in my mailbox—court hearing notices, copies of evaluations and court records, new petitions filed, and demands for payment. But I was doing well at work, despite my chaotic personal life.

One day, I was temporarily transferred to the publications department to write test procedures because work in the test department had slowed down. I realized, even at the time, that my boss loaned me out primarily because I was a woman, and in that era, most men never questioned the assumption that all women were born knowing how to type. Except me. I had only taken an Introduction to Typing course in junior high, so I wasn't very good at entering data on a keyboard.

I was grateful for his sexism, though, because after only a few days, I realized that I had found my calling. I requested a transfer to technical publications and applied for a permanent position as a writer/editor. I was offered the job, which came with a higher salary, and I jumped at the opportunity.

Clark continued to work as well. He was out on bail, so the bail bond was another expense we had to pay. He worked at the University of Colorado in the Veterans' Affairs (VA) office advising military veterans about their VA benefits.

After my suicide attempt, I experienced a lot of conflicting feelings about God. I was thankful that He saved me, and at the same time, angry with Him for saving me. I was sure He didn't exist, then I would find myself praying, which I did a lot during the trial.

God, do you care about us?

-30-

The Verdict is In

◻◇●◇◻

THE DAY OF THE verdict came. We all squeezed into the courtroom. Clark was at the defense table with his lawyer. I was sitting directly behind him.

The foreman handed a piece of paper to the judge. After glancing at the paper, the judge handed it back to the foreman, who loudly read:

"We—the people of the jury—find the defendant... not guilty."

Not guilty. NOT guilty! NOT GUILTY! I collapsed with relief. Before the judge dismissed the jury, he told them they were now free to talk about the trial.

Several members of the jury came over to where Clark and I stood and, with tears in their eyes, told us how sorry they were that we had been subjected to this nightmare. I was in shock. For so long, I had believed that everyone hated us and would never see us as anything but child abusers. I was so shocked at their reaction, I just stood there and cried.

Not long after the trial, our attorney asked members of the jury if he could interview them. This is a common practice. Attorneys learn from the juries what strategies worked and what didn't so they can hone their tactics in future cases.

Afterwards, Phil said the jurors told him that five minutes into deliberations, they decided to take a poll. Eleven out of the twelve jurors voted not guilty. The twelfth juror said she wasn't sure because she wondered if there was something the prosecution hadn't presented, maybe something he'd been prevented from presenting by some ruling from the judge.

I think she watched too many crime dramas on TV. The other jurors finally convinced her that they couldn't base a decision on conjecture about something that wasn't presented, and after a couple of hours, she relented.

Everything was great then, right? They returned Emily after Clark was found "not guilty?"

And once again, the answer is a big fat "Nope!!"

The DSS Dependency and Neglect case was not affected by the "not guilty" verdict in Clark's trial. Does that make sense to you? Would it make sense to anybody? If he was not guilty of abuse, how could I be guilty of not protecting Emily from someone who *wasn't* abusing her?

Maybe it will make more sense after I tell you what the DSS told us, "Just because Clark was found not guilty in criminal court, it doesn't mean he's innocent."

Since the burden of proof was not as high in civil cases as it was in criminal cases, the status of the civil case related to the criminal case remained unaffected. If the DSS decided they wanted to continue to pursue it, they could.

And—of course they did. They were just getting started with their revenge against me for not siding with them in the first place.

So, it was with joy and occasional bouts of heart-stopping terror that I met the news in late November that we were going to have another child.

Yes, I was pregnant.

The Dependency and Neglect case brought against me by the DSS continued unabated throughout that Christmas holiday season. Clark's success at trial only made them even more determined to punish me for daring to disagree with their conclusions and recommendations.

I felt like a piñata, swinging back and forth with each blow, helpless to change my circumstances or avoid the "beatings" I was getting. I wondered if I would ever be free from this alien attack force. They wanted to permanently remove my custody rights regarding Emily and prevent Clark from ever being alone with her.

Why they never bothered to include Amber in any of their petitions was a mystery to me. If I was a bad mother to Emily, why wasn't I a bad mother to Amber? I didn't want to rock the boat by asking the question, though, and I was glad they left her alone.

Most of the time, Clark and I focused on the excitement of having a baby instead of thinking about the DSS. We endlessly discussed names. In 1986, a baby's gender could not be determined before birth, and we finally settled on the name Carson, a unisex name. We were excited, yes, but I had moments of extreme anxiety over what could happen. Would the DSS be standing outside my hospital room during the baby's birth, just waiting to remove Carson, too? These thoughts kept me on edge much of the time.

The stress continued to mount. Three days before the Dependency and Neglect hearing in February of 1987, I had a checkup with the obstetrician. Our unborn baby had died.

I was shocked and heartbroken.

I gave up. I was depressed and beaten and couldn't fight any more. Too many beautiful parts of my life had been stolen from me in the previous twelve months and replaced with ugly lies and ruthless vindictiveness.

I'd experienced so much emotional trauma in such a short time that I accepted most of the conditions in the petition in exchange for a dismissal of the case against me. I signed the agreement, and at the hearing, the case against me was dismissed.

Immediately after the hearing, I was admitted to the hospital for surgery to remove Carson and say goodbye to our unborn child.

□◇●◇□

The terms of the agreement I'd signed in exchange for dismissing the case included certain stipulations: I would continue to have joint custody of Amber, but permanent legal custody of Emily would be awarded to Daryl. I would be given supervised visitation under oversight by Beth Lieberman, the appointed mental health professional, but there would be no contact between Emily and Clark during these visits or at any other time.

The stated goal was to work toward normal reasonable visitation between Emily and me, without restrictions on the presence or absence of Clark. Beth Lieberman was the therapist appointed by the court to be the arbiter of when normal visitation could occur. She would also control the court-ordered treatment plan and therapy schedule.

We insisted on including another clause, however, because I was suspicious that Lieberman would drag this process out far beyond a reasonable length of time. If any party felt the resumption toward "normal visitation" was too slow or too fast, that party was allowed to seek and pay for a second opinion to evaluate the progress and treatment plan.

I am the kind of person who can make a joke out of almost any event, and I wish I could say something humorous about this period in my life to lighten the retelling of this sad story, but... I've got nothing. It was very, very sad.

My relationship with God also hit the rocks. I continued to have conflicting feelings. *Should I pray? Why even bother? Was God even real?* He had rejected so many of my pleas in the past year—with the exception of Clark's acquittal—that I was beginning to wonder, question, and seriously doubt.

I finally settled on one way to relate to God.

I said, "God, if you really exist, you are going to have to show me—prove it to me. If you can't do that, I'm not going to believe in you anymore."

My faith was decimated. I had come to the end of myself.

Then I stopped praying, stopped believing, stopped going to church, stopped talking about God—I stopped everything.

I just stopped.

-31-

Picking Up the Pieces

ᵒ◇●◇ᵒ

I FOUND MY SENSE of humor again and have to repeat a joke that comedian Christopher Titus tells about his acrimonious divorce.

> *People said to me, "You weren't meant to be together. It was God's will."*
>
> *Really? God's will? God got involved in this? Twenty years of my life gone? All the money I made, the career I chose, pretty much torn to pieces? Two little kids' lives shattered?*
>
> *Really God? Is **THAT** how you work?! This brutal, disemboweling nightmare is **YOU?!!** Because if that's the case, **THEN THERE IS NO GOD!!!!***
>
> *And God said unto me...*[5]

I love that joke. It reminds me that even if we scream in frustration that God doesn't exist, it won't deter God from continuing to speak to us. He keeps talking, whether we are listening or not.

When I gave my ultimatum to God, it was months before I heard even a squeak from Him, at least a squeak that I could understand. It took me time to tune into His frequency again. He was talking. I just wasn't hearing it.

126

We were angry from the false accusation and distressed by the amount of money we had to continue to pay for legal fees, psychotherapy sessions, and court costs.

A few weeks after the hearing, we began collecting information to pursue a lawsuit as recommended by the judge's law partner in his letter to our attorney concerning the rejected plea bargain.

After our attorney reviewed all the material, we got this assessment from him.

> *"I do not believe you have a viable legal claim against any of the persons involved in your prosecution. The reason is that all of them are cloaked in the doctrine of sovereign immunity. Although arguments could be made to attempt to get around that doctrine, I can find no such argument which I believe to be viable."*

I had to look up "sovereign immunity" in the legal dictionary, and here's what it said.

> *"Sovereign immunity is a judicial doctrine that prevents the government or its political subdivisions, departments, or agencies from being sued without its consent. The doctrine stems from the ancient English principle that the monarch can do no wrong."*

Well, it CAN do wrong, as I've so thoroughly illustrated in the last several chapters! But we knew the people involved in our cases would never agree to allow us to sue them.

The system wins again.

A few months after I signed the agreement to have the charges dismissed against me, Emily recanted, i.e., "took back" the whole story of sexual abuse and said as much to her therapist, Beth Lieberman. Here's an excerpt from the therapist's report to the court where Lieberman describes it.

> *Emily believes that the DSS asked her leading questions implying that she had been molested, and she felt she had to affirm their references. She also states*

that once she had done so, she was reluctant to let anyone know that these events did not take place because she was afraid [she] "would get in trouble."

To comply with the agreement I signed, we went to court-ordered therapy. So much therapy! Sessions with Emily; sessions without Emily; sessions with Daryl, Pam, Emily, and the therapist; sessions with Clark, me, and the therapist; sessions with Clark, me, Amber, Emily, and the therapist. You get the idea.

I became more and more depressed. I still hadn't heard enough "squeaking" from God to believe He cared about what was happening.

When we reached the one-year mark of therapy in February of 1988, another report was due from Lieberman to the court.

With all this therapy coming out of our ears, this was likely enough therapy. And the next stage would be reintegration of Emily into our lives without supervision. At least that's what I thought.

But what did the report recommend?

More therapy.

Yep, that's what she recommended. More therapy.

In the report, Lieberman points out at least three good reasons to get out of our lives forever.

She concludes, however, that two years of counseling with her—*forty-eight sessions*—isn't enough to put a family back together that should never have been torn apart in the first place.

Excerpt from letter dated Feb. 16, 1988:

(1) Emily's relationship with each parent has improved in the areas of open communication of feelings and in Emily's comfort with herself and each parent.

(2) Emily has recanted her allegations of sexual abuse against her stepfather, Clark Gabriel, and at this point has consistently maintained this posture for a number of months.

*(3) Emily strongly wishes to re-initiate her relation-
ship with her mother on a more consistent basis, and
to re-initiate her relationship with her stepfather,
Clark Gabriel. Emily has also expressed a wish to
have more consistent and frequent contact with her
sister, Amber, who will in all likelihood be going
away to college this fall.*

*(4) Despite the expression of these wishes on Emily's
part, she is still viewed by this therapist as pos-
sessing fragile ego strength, significant anxiety concerning the implementation of her renewed
relationship with her mother and stepfather, and
vulnerable to regression if these steps are mishan-
dled.*

She went on to recommend that Emily continue psychotherapy through June 15, 1988. At that time, she would provide
an updated report.

ARRGH!!! Lieberman's report was the last straw. Emily was
now eleven years old! We had missed out on two years of her
life because of the system's overzealousness, vindictiveness,
and greed.

The alien spaceship took another orbit around the strange
planet that was *not* earth and dropped us on our heads again.

Clark and I located another therapist, explained the situation,
and he met with Emily. Afterwards, the new therapist wrote
his own opinion and recommendation, which he submitted to
the court on May 15, 1988:

*It is my opinion that Emily has benefited from ther-
apy, is capable of making a competent decision
about spending more time with her mother and stepfather, is psychologically ready to do so and would
not be psychologically damaged as a result of any
contact. She expresses much eagerness to reestablish
a relationship with her stepfather and demonstrated
much affection and closeness with her mother. What
little pain that is currently being expressed in her
family relationships is focused on her stepmother.*

He then went on to recommend only one more family session with Beth Lieberman followed by unsupervised visits with both Clark and me. We were thrilled. Even though I still didn't have custody like I did before the DSS took Emily, at least she could finally spend a couple of weekends a month with us.

On my way to pick up Emily for our first unsupervised visit together, I was scanning through the radio stations when my ear picked up something. I stopped scanning.

> *Fear them not, therefore; for there is nothing covered that shall not be revealed; and hid that shall not be known.*[6]

Those words came through to me like I had a loudspeaker in the car.

While driving, I'd been thinking about how frustrating it was that we couldn't sue the child protection system. They were going to be able to keep tearing apart families without repercussions.

This Bible verse seemed to be countering that assumption. I remembered that verse from my Bible-reading past and repeated the verse a few times in my head. If this was my first "squeak" from God, I would eventually know because only God could oversee a solution that was powerful enough to expose what they had done and stop them from continuing to do it.

Dear God, if you're there, please help us expose this evil.

-32-

All's Fair in War

◻◇●◇◻

A FTER WE LEARNED the child protection system couldn't be sued, we began to learn as much as we could about the problems in the system.

We learned that the child abuse laws in each state were altered in response to the cultural war against child abuse that began in the late 1970s.

(1) Federal financial assistance was given to the states if they changed their child abuse laws to meet certain requirements, including "enhanced mandated reporting."

(2) Enhanced mandated reporting required people to report suspected cases of child abuse or face prosecution while— at the same time—it gave people immunity from a lawsuit or prosecution if they wrongly or maliciously reported abuse.

(3) Child sexual abuse cases were more aggressively pursued as a result of increased funds set aside for this purpose.

Thus began our nightmare.

The agencies were in full swing of "extreme child protection" by the time they caught us in their nets in 1986.

But we began to wonder—if we can't sue them, can we raise awareness about what they did to us? What would happen if we focused a megawatt spotlight on this overreach in the

131

name of protecting children? Maybe there are even other families who've been torn apart for no reason like we were.

Can we make it harder in the future for them to do to other families what they did to us?

We realized it was a long shot since the system was so powerful and we were nobodies. Worse than that, we were nobodies facing an even bigger stumbling block. We had been prosecuted as child abusers, and the prevailing assumption that no one seemed to question was, "children never lie about abuse."

So—who would believe us?

Did I really want to have to endlessly counter the statement that was offered as proof of our guilt, "Where there's smoke there's fire"?

I absolutely hated to be the center of attention—even positive attention—did I really want to continue being the center of negative attention?

I went over every argument in my mind—both pro and con—about the wisdom of taking on a system that was so huge and powerful.

But every time I thought about what the system had done to our family, I felt such anger that I could barely contain it. My reputation was already in tatters. What difference would more attention make? Emily was still gone. Amber would be going off to college soon so it wouldn't affect her future. And poor Carson never had the chance to even draw a breath.

In the end, I couldn't stop myself from doing something, no matter what other people thought of me. Every day that Emily was held captive was one more day I spent researching the topic, writing letters to the editor, and talking about it to anyone who would listen.

I found statistics such as, in 1983, the percentage of reported cases of sexual maltreatment in Colorado was more than twice the percentage of cases reported for the entire country. l used these kinds of statistics, along with other data, journal articles, and professional statements to strengthen my arguments.

Then I discovered V.O.C.A.L., Victims of Child Abuse Laws. Yes—Victims of Child Abuse *Laws* —not victims of child abuse.

V.O.C.A.L. was several organizations, if you count each state chapter as a separate organization—that fought against the over-zealous child protection system. We weren't the only people in the country who were caught in this spider web. I ran across a contact phone number for a V.O.C.A.L. Chapter in Minnesota and contacted them. I spoke with a woman named Margaret (Peg), who founded the Minnesota Chapter of V.O.C.A.L. in 1984.

Peg sent me a lot of information, news, and professional journal articles, which included a story about how she had started the Minnesota V.O.C.A.L. group. She also sent me names and phone numbers for V.O.C.A.L. points of contact in a few other states. I contacted each one. Some phone numbers were no longer in service. I made a notation next to each number— whom I spoke with and what we discussed.

One day our local paper, the *Colorado Springs Gazette Telegraph*, printed a "Letter to the Editor" that I wrote about the child protection system's problems, and I was thrilled.

Not long after the letter appeared in the newspaper, I started getting phone calls and letters from people in the area who had experiences similar to ours.

It was time to organize a support group. I put an announcement in the newspaper, and we held the first meeting in our home. Ten people attended.

Dear God, if you're there please help us in this fight.

Greater is He

As things go from bad to worse,
it seems to me that we are cursed
with constant arguments and strife.
Can't we just enjoy this life
without the painful misalignments
caused by Satan's vile defiance?

Satan tried to challenge God
and lured mankind by way of fraud,
using falsehoods, tricks and lies
to orchestrate our sad demise.

Will you let his reign continue?
Or employ all that's within you?
With God's spirit we can lead
with love and see the hate recede,
binding Satan to the wall
and ending this mad free-for-all.

-33-

Raising Our Voices

□◇●◇□

IN THE FALL OF 1987, we started our very own V.O.C.A.L. chapter. After researching how to form a non-profit organization in the State of Colorado, Clark completed and submitted the paperwork. Now we would have to wait and see if the application was approved, which could take months.

In the meantime, additional people who had their own horror stories about the child protection system contacted us, and together we pooled ideas on how to better support victims of the overzealous caseworkers and prosecutors and reach a wider audience to demand change.

We exchanged information about "good" professionals we had discovered—lawyers, psychotherapists, and others who approached the issues objectively. From this information, we created a list that we could use for referrals. On our list, we wanted professionals who understood that occasionally the system mistakenly—or even sometimes vindictively—pursued abuse cases and harmed families.

Clark and I started a newsletter that included our referral list, book reviews, reprinted articles, and original pieces. I frequently wrote about the nightmare other group members were going through, using aliases and changing a few other details to respect their privacy.

Since the internet and email were not available back in 1987, we "snail-mailed" our newsletter to everyone who contacted us. We also enclosed copies of our newsletter every time we wrote a letter to the media or a state legislator.

Finally, our efforts started paying off. In late 1987, I was contacted by a member of the Colorado Springs Chapter of the Colorado Press Association, a trade organization for the news media, and was invited to speak at their local chapter meeting.

I agreed to do it but was terrified spitless. Public speaking has never been my strength. I was much better at writing, obviously, since that was how I came to their attention in the first place.

I wrote a speech, practiced it, and figured I had no choice. I just hoped I wouldn't be totally paralyzed by fear like I was in seventh grade speech class.

As I was driving to the meeting, I wondered if praying would help. Out of the blue, a Bible verse I learned back during my church-going days popped into my head.

> But when they hand you over, do not worry about what you are to say, for it will be given to you in that hour.[7]

All I could do was pray that the right words would be given to me at the right time.

I would like to tell you that I spoke like a disciple spreading the gospel or like Martin Luther King, Jr. in his famous "I Have a Dream" speech.

Unfortunately, I can't.

I probably did ok, but I'm sure my discomfort was obvious. As I spoke, I looked at the audience and saw a lot of faces staring back at me with expressions ranging from doubt to actual distaste.

Their expressions did nothing to help calm my nerves or improve my speech delivery.

When I opened the floor for questions, I got some questions obviously designed to throw me off my game. And I'm not sure

I gave great answers. But what they didn't know was that they were giving me practice.

Hard questions now gave me the opportunity to prepare more persuasive responses for future speeches and interviews. I was only going to get better and better.

Then it was over. I breathed a sigh of relief and looked for a quick exit.

A couple of people approached and asked if they could interview me for an article. I was surprised and at first thought I'd made headway, then I immediately became suspicious.

I said I might be interested and left it at that. They had my contact information.

The bad part about being interviewed for this article, I thought, *is not knowing how they might slant my statements to fit their narrative.*

I was right to be suspicious. The next day one of the meeting attendees called me and said she was writing an article about an abuse and neglect case I'd read about in the paper the day before. She said she wanted an opinion from "the other side."

The previous evening, I thought long and hard about the questions asked during the press club meeting and how to answer them. I was ready with my response.

> *If you're looking for an opinion from 'the other side,' you're talking to the wrong person. You need to find a group that believes children should be abused, because that would be the 'other side' of the debate. We do not condone abuse of children in any way, and, in fact, are opposed to ALL abuse, including the abuse that happens when children are ripped from loving homes and placed into foster care without adequate investigations first.*

Then she asked the other question that I heard over and over. "How do you know that people who come to V.O.C.A.L. to get help aren't guilty of abuse?"

I told her that we didn't judge because there was no way of knowing who was guilty and who wasn't. I also said that we didn't offer a way to help guilty people "get off." We were just a support organization for people who felt wronged by the system.

I said that we advised people to talk to their attorneys, but if they were guilty of the charges, caseworkers would likely work with them to reunify their family more quickly if they admitted guilt than if they said they were innocent.

Then I gave her my personal account of how I still didn't have Emily back home, nearly two years after they took her, even though Clark had been found not guilty at trial.

I figured this wasn't the kind of "comment from the other side" they were looking for and doubted if they would print it. But I checked the newspaper the next day, and they did.

Although it was short and didn't go into depth, they at least printed a few sentences, my name, and the name of V.O.C.A.L. Score one for us!

More publicity.

Dear God, thank you for helping us draw attention to these problems.

-34-

Higher and Higher

□◇●◇□

L ESS THAN A WEEK later, I had the opportunity to again promote our group and our issues with the system when a local talk show was discussing the same abuse case that was in the newspaper. I dialed and dialed and dialed but couldn't get into the talk show line.

I decided to send a fax instead. I typed up my comments about the case and information about V.O.C.A.L. and faxed it to them.

That afternoon, someone from the radio show called and asked if I would like to be interviewed for a few minutes during the show the next morning. And like that, we were off to the races!

The following week, I was contacted by the producer of a local cable TV show called *One World,* and I did an hour-long interview that was taped for a later airing.

Our phone started ringing much more frequently, sometimes at odd hours of the night, and Clark came up with the idea of getting an 800 phone number, something that would be easier for people to remember when we gave it out.

He called the phone company, and by the time he was done, he had secured the perfect phone number for us: 1-800-84-V.O.C.A.L., a tribute to George Orwell's dystopian novel written in 1949 about the "future" year 1984. Orwell predicted the advent of "thought police," redefined words, and ubiquitous government surveillance and control, which reminded us of our experience with the Child Protection System (CPS).

Clark's name had been added to Colorado's State Registry of Perpetrators of Child Sexual Assault in May 1986, before he even went to trial. Getting his name expunged from this registry was important to his future, as it could affect his employment opportunities. It was also one more arrow in CPS's quiver if they ever decided to bring new charges against him and one more stranglehold they had on due process.

"Innocent until proven guilty" seemed to be an outdated concept when it involved child abuse. People accused of a child abuse crime were considered guilty forever and deserved all the mud that could be slung at them. No trial was needed.

To get his name expunged from the registry, we had to petition the court and meet a specific burden of proof to show that the event didn't happen. Our attorney told us it wouldn't be easy to get the record expunged because the standard of proof needed to keep his name on the registry was the lowest level.

If a judge felt that it was more likely than not that Clark really had abused Emily, his name would not be removed from the registry. But we added this task to our already growing list, and finally got his name removed from the State's Registry.

◻◇●◇◻

Also in 1987, Clark finally talked me into changing majors and changing schools. He still worked at the Colorado Springs campus of the University of Colorado.

I submitted my application and was accepted. For some reason, the fact that I wouldn't be able to have a 4.0 GPA when I graduated didn't seem to be as important anymore.

It was easy to select my major: psychology.

Clark's college major was business, but he still had to take a few electives. We decided to take a few classes together, including a sociology class one semester and a psychology class the following semester.

We had fun taking those classes together.

In fact, so much fun, I'm sure the professors breathed a sigh of relief when the semesters were over. We'd learned the art of questioning assumptions that were presented as known facts in a field that was anything but certain and settled truth.

Hopefully we caused others to think more critically, too.

◻◇●◇◻

Amber dated Marty until the fall of 1987 when he left for college to attend Tulane University. Amber was still a senior at Fountain Valley Academy and would graduate in the spring of 1988.

At least I hoped so. After some of the phone calls I received from the school, there was some doubt. She had the most distinct privilege of being on Fountain Valley's Honor Roll and, at the same time, on the list of students who might not be allowed to graduate.

Amber was at Fountain Valley on scholarship, one she'd been awarded after applying for it in ninth grade and writing the winning essay. We didn't know about it until after she'd won since she failed to mention it to us when she applied.

Only two full-tuition scholarships were awarded each year to this exclusive and expensive prep school academy—one to a boy and one to a girl. She began attending the school in her sophomore year.

Although Amber did well in the classes, she ran into a few issues because, unlike her fellow students, she did not have millionaire parents.

The first issue was the required special project students had to complete during spring break each year. The school sent home a list of recommended activities to fulfill this graduation requirement.

Parents were required to foot the bill. The choices involved long-distance trips and activities, such as,

(1) Write a report about your experience on an African safari and discuss Africa's animal preservation policies.

(2) Interview Alaskan natives on a trip to Juneau and write a report on their lifestyle.

(3) Research bird species commonly found in Peru and create a photo journal of your trip.

The approximate cost for each activity was listed in the brochure Amber brought home. Each one listed was far beyond our budget.

Being a creative and clever girl, Amber wrote a proposal to the school to suggest that scholarship students be allowed to develop and participate in an activity of their own choice that would cost nothing.

Her proposed activity was to intern for two weeks at a local TV station and write about the experience. The school appreciated her creative resourcefulness and accepted her proposal.

Throughout her tenure at Fountain Valley, Amber was required to participate in something we found unusual that was called Sit-Down Dinner. Students were required to eat dinner together once a week and demonstrate proper table manners and behavior while having dinner.

Normal people like us just eat. We try not to pick our noses at the table or eat with our fingers unless we're eating pizza or fried chicken.

We eat this way because our parents put food on our highchair trays when we were toddlers, and we eventually figured out how to get the food mostly into our mouths. We didn't have to take a class in school to learn how to eat.

So right off the bat, we didn't take this requirement very seriously. However, the school did. And the fact that Amber had a job on weekends and often didn't have free time to attend Sit-Down Dinners wasn't an adequate excuse.

I remember one call in particular. I was at work. I listened to their concerns, then applied my newly acquired sociology professor-approved vocabulary and recently learned Rogerian psychotherapy techniques to express my understanding of the issue and empathize with their concerns.

I said, "Amber is bright and creative, but challenging to mainstream," among other intellectual-sounding statements.

I apparently said the right things, however, because they backed off and said they understood about their less fortunate students' monetary needs to hold down a job. I felt partly offended, but mostly amused and pleased that my insincere performance had worked.

Early in her senior year, Amber applied for admission to Columbia University in New York. She was not only admitted, but earned early admission, a highly prized status. She was also eligible for grants and loans that would pay for the tuition, plus room and board.

She was thrilled. I was proud but a little concerned with the culture shock she was bound to experience. A middle-class neighborhood in Colorado Springs to an Ivy League college in New York City was a gigantic leap into a foreign culture.

Amber's relationship with Clark continued to improve. In 1988, when she was old enough to legally consent, she asked Clark to adopt her. And he did.

In June of 1988, Amber graduated from Fountain Valley Academy.

And we all breathed a sigh of relief!

We had just won unrestricted visitation with Emily, so when Emily came to Amber's graduation, we were thrilled to see her.

It was wonderful to have Emily visit on weekends. She was able to rekindle her relationship with, not only Clark, but also Amber, which had been badly damaged by the separation. This was a serious side effect that no one in the child protection system ever considered or cared about, except for a question once raised by a family court judge during one hearing.

"Is keeping the siblings apart affecting their relationship?"

The child savers ignored the question, and the judge never asked it again. More proof that their stated goals were directly at odds with their actions.

Dear God, thank you for helping Amber adjust and thank you for letting Emily come visit us!

-35-

The New V.O.C.A.L. Majority

◻◇●◇◻

V.O.C.A.L. SOUTHERN COLORADO was officially designated as a non-profit organization in June 1988. Clark had listed the two of us on the application as members of V.O.C.A.L.'s board of directors to fulfill a requirement of the State.

Now when I sent out letters or spoke to groups or on talk shows, I could refer to myself as being "on the board of directors" of V.O.C.A.L. Southern Colorado, which sounded like someone who had more clout than I actually did. I hoped it would add more weight to what I was saying.

By this time, our organization had grown to 30 or 40 local people and included several hard-working member volunteers who sent out packets of information and counseled people in person or on the phone. We rented a small office and a copier that would handle the volume of pages we were producing and give people a place to meet.

Clark and I were still footing the majority of the organization's expenses, although we did get some additional contributions once the organization achieved non-profit status.

But we also decided to start a typesetting and graphic design business to help pay for the expenses, and we worked with owners of weekly newspapers and advertisers to design and typeset their printed products.

144

In the fall of 1988, a writer from *Ms. Magazine,* a national women's magazine that was sold in grocery store checkout stands and also via subscriptions, called to ask me for an interview. She said they were doing a story on the problems in the child protection system.

I was thrilled, excited, and nervous. This was a new milestone. We had finally attracted national attention! She asked lots of questions, and, to support my recounting of the events, I agreed to send her reports and copies of court documents from my own case.

As I stood in front of the copier watching the sheets feed through, I happened to glance at the bulletin board that hung above the copier. I noticed a new sheet of paper tacked to the spot where Connie, one of our most dedicated volunteers, often left quotes or Bible verses to inspire the rest of us. I stopped and stared at the new Bible verse she had tacked up:

> *Fear them not, therefore; for there is nothing covered that shall not be revealed; and hid that shall not be known. Luke 12:2 KJV*

My mouth went dry as I remembered the day I heard those words amplified by my car radio speakers. It was the day I drove to pick up Emily for her first unrestricted visit a few months before.

Is this you, God? Are you trying to tell me that you are in this somehow?

I still wasn't quite sure what to believe. Coincidence? Or God?

To our immense relief and satisfaction, *Ms. Magazine* prominently featured our family's story, with a teaser on the cover and an article that spanned several pages. We were pleased to see that the article credibly explained the harmful actions of the child protection system and the effects their overzealous pursuits had on families.

The only problem, if you could call it a problem, was that the magazine had printed our 800 number at the end of the article.

Our phone rang from the moment the magazines hit mailboxes until—well, until—three chapters from now. I would use the phrase "sun-up to sundown" except it didn't stop at sundown. It continued to ring. All day and, it would have been all night, until we realized that we had to shut the ringer off or we'd never get any sleep.

But we didn't leave our callers without recourse. We recorded a message that directed people to leave their addresses if they wanted information mailed, their phone number if they needed to speak to a V.O.C.A.L. volunteer, or a message after the beep for anything else.

Unfortunately, many people were so desperate to tell us about their stories in their voicemail messages, we had to frequently take note of the messages and immediately delete them to make room for more. Hearing these stories, many of them at least as tragic as our own, just made my resolve that much stronger to expose this abuse in the name of protecting children.

We were overwhelmed, both with the volume of calls and the volume of alleged false accusations of child abuse. Over the next few months, we did the best we could to keep up, returning calls, making copies of our information packets, and mailing them out—but it was truly more than we were able to manage well.

Some people were irritated about our slow response, but most people were understanding and just grateful for any support or information we could give them.

We referred people in other states to the other organizations we knew about, and I was glad that we had been keeping track of contact information for the other groups. We were able to help a lot more people that way.

The *Ms. Magazine* article's publication sparked an explosion of interest on several other fronts. The Director of our county's Department of Social Services, Bob VanCleave, was now willing to meet with Clark and me to discuss our experience with the system.

I wasn't certain whether this was some sort of trick or a sincere desire to hear what happened to us so he could reevaluate their approach, but we prepared as best we could and met with him.

Bob surprised me on two fronts: (1) his openness to hearing about our complaints and (2) his almost total ignorance about the problems that had been and were continuing to be caused by caseworkers.

But when I learned that he hadn't been the director during the time that Emily was removed from our home and had only become the director in 1988, I understood his lack of knowledge about it.

He asked lots of questions, but I could tell by the way he asked them that he doubted at least part of what we told him.

However, what sane person wouldn't? It was a bizarre story. I agreed to send him documents to bolster our version of the experience, and he agreed to read them and look into our allegations of mistreatment by his department.

Colorado was definitely not the only state with big problems. Over the next several months we received calls from every state in the U.S. We'd built up a contact list that included people in V.O.C.A.L. or similar organizations in every state, as well as several in Canada.

Books and professional journal articles about false allegations were also starting to appear, and we offered the books and notebooks filled with articles for a donation to V.O.C.A.L. Some cases reached national media attention, but none more so than a case in California that took place in a preschool owned by Virginia McMartin in the Los Angeles area.[8]

Members of the family, who operated the preschool, were accused of bizarre acts that read like a horror story. They were charged with 115 counts of child abuse, which was later expanded to 321 counts involving 48 children. Allegations included witches flying, secret tunnels under the school, orgies in airports, and children flushed down the toilet.[9]

The trial itself lasted an unbelievable *seven years* and cost $15 million, the longest and most expensive criminal case in the history of the United States legal system. And the end result? *No convictions.*[10]

Michael P. Maloney, a clinical psychologist and professor of psychiatry, testified during the trial as an expert witness, and his testimony had great impact on the jury. He reviewed videotapes of the children's interviews, which he called "improper, coercive, directive, problematic and adult-directed in a way that forced the children to follow a rigid script." He concluded that "many of the kids' statements in the interviews were generated by the examiner."[11]

After our experience of being flooded with calls from all over the country and directing people to our network of V.O.C.A.L. organizations, Clark came up with the idea of adding a new name to our non-profit organization: V.O.C.A.L. National Network (VNN). We adopted a new mission statement that included expanding the reach of our organization to a national level to further the goal of reforming the child protection system.

We introduced the new name in the fall of 1988. We liked it because it took the word "victim" out of the organization's name.

We didn't feel like "victims" anymore. We felt like "warriors."

And I was beginning to sense God's presence in our lives once again. It started simply, with just a few Bible verses recalled once in a while that fit a circumstance perfectly.

As I continued to tune my senses, I would more frequently recall a relevant Bible verse or hear a random song lyric or quote that answered a question I'd been pondering. This happened more and more frequently, so I began to seek God out.

I resumed praying, reading the Bible, and listening to Christian music. My mistrust collapsed, and I saw that God had been there the whole time. helping us at every turn.

I also realized that the severe emotional turmoil I'd experienced was caused, not by God's abandonment, but rather, by my own lack of trust. I hadn't really believed that God was in control, and I let fear overtake me with each new setback.

Now I know that God is here with me, no matter how dire the circumstance. And I know that God loves us.

Dear God, please keep talking. I want to know you better.

◻◇●◇◻

Thou Are the Potter

I will shape this poem
like a potter shapes his bowl,
like our Father shapes us, too,
into something truly bold,
into something strong and free,
into something we could never be
without the gifts he gives to us
of love and true forgiveness.
Jesus if You stay by me
and help me heed the call,
when I have a job to do,
together, we'll stand tall.

Help me bravely fight in battle.
Help me swim when floods arise.
Help me be the one who will,
for others, sacrifice.
Jesus, You gave all for us
I'll gladly follow with my trust
in You because I'd surely fail
when hit with the first gusty gale.
With Your strength and wisdom, too,
I'll work until the job is through.
My goal is not to disappoint,
but boldly move when You anoint.

-36-

Shouting Down the Walls of Jericho

◻◇●◇◻

I N 1988, WE RECEIVED a phone call from someone named Richard Wexler. He'd read about our case in the Ms. Magazine article and was wondering if he could interview us for his book. He was also looking for additional families to interview who had similar experiences and asked if we could give him any other names of people harmed by the system.

Yes! In fact, we had a whole slew of names! And yes, of course we would be happy to be interviewed for the book. It was a huge opportunity!

Richard interviewed Clark and me on the phone, asked for Daryl and Pam's contact information so he could interview them. He also wanted to interview our lawyer, as well as Emily and Amber. We sent him copies of court records, psychiatric evaluations, and DSS interview notes.

It would be months before the book came out, and in the meantime, we had our own publishing to do. We turned our newsletter into a magazine and called it *V.O.C.A.L. Perspective*. The first issue was printed on coated paper stock and saddle stitched, just like a regular magazine. It came out in February of 1989, three years to the day after they took Emily.

The magazine was twenty-eight pages, not including front and back cover. We were so proud of it! Like parents of a newborn with photos galore, we had so many copies of that issue printed that I still have copies today.

The magazine included original articles, articles reprinted with permission, opinion pieces, book reviews, and a heart-rending section called "Letters Home" that was inspired by letters Emily wrote to me when she wasn't allowed to come home.

I loved the piece Clark wrote about the issue's cover:

All too often a parent is labeled guilty before he or she is even tried in court. The stigma of being branded—in spite of our judicial system's standard of "innocent until proven guilty"—sometimes over-comes even the strongest person.

Not only do the parents feel shame and frustration, but friends and relatives are thinking, "They must be guilty. Why were they accused if they weren't?"

The rubber stamp reads GUILTY. You soon learn that proving innocence isn't possible; the best verdict you can hope for is not guilty.

Not until the emotions and finances are exhausted does the system sometimes admit that evidence is lacking. Unfortunately, it's too late. The child's birth-days have come and gone; Christmases weren't merry. So-called friends have abandoned you; rela-tives speak of you but not to you.... You get the NOT stamped over the GUILTY, but in everyone's mind, there is no certainty.

The illusion looks very real to most people.

The pain you've experienced, however, is no illu-sion.[12]

In the spring of 1989, a miracle occurred.

Daryl called and asked if Emily could come back and live with me again. I was floored! He'd fought me so hard when everyone thought Clark was guilty, I couldn't believe his change of heart!

I asked him why he changed his mind, and he said something about Emily being hard to handle. Then he seemed to think better of it, and he said only that Emily missed me, and they thought she would do better if she were living with me again.

Of course, I said yes. I was thrilled! After more than three years without her, I finally got my daughter back! Emily moved back in with us that weekend, and we all celebrated. Our family was finally dropped back on earth, and the aliens were on the run.

The next *V.O.C.A.L. Perspective* issue was thirty-two pages and was released in the summer of 1989. The first issue of the magazine had been a hit, and in the second issue, we printed twelve letters to the editor, which was gratifying. It meant that people had read the magazine and were motivated to respond. Several articles, interviews, and personal stories were in the second issue, including one I wrote called, "Alan in Wonderland," which was based on the experience of one of our members—a high school teacher who had been maliciously accused of abuse by a student.

That fall, we came out with our third issue. It was thirty-six pages and included a photo on the cover of Bob VanCleave, the DSS Director, whom we'd invited to speak to our V.O.C.A.L. group about his newly formed Quality Assurance Program.

A few weeks before he spoke to the group, Bob had asked Clark to participate in a Citizens' Advisory Committee that he was establishing to deal with the problems in the DSS.

Bob's presentation included several insightful points, such as this response to a question about what had prompted him to form a Quality Assurance Program.

A series of things happened. One was the sense I got when talking to a number of you in this room, a large number of you.

I didn't have any way of knowing the validity of the complaints. But I read some of the cases. I've looked at the caseworker's story and what I became impressed with was that, even if I could take the most conservative stance in favor of our department and say, "We were right one hundred percent of the time," how is it then that people were so motivated to come and talk to me?

They felt so discounted, they felt so unimportant, they felt so disgusting in the eyes of the people who worked for me, that they were motivated to come to me. And that's assuming all our decisions are always right.

I knew then that we had to do something. Bureaucracies, in and of themselves, typically don't make themselves vulnerable. In fact, they do the opposite, the walls get higher and higher.[ii]

We held a national V.O.C.A.L. conference in 1990 and lined up several well-known experts in the field to give speeches and presentations. The conference was well-attended.

That winter, members of our V.O.C.A.L. organization were given the opportunity to testify in front of the Colorado State Legislature about their concerns over the State's child abuse laws that allowed the system to ravage families and destroy lives.

Several legislators were now exposed to the problems we saw in the state's child abuse laws. And a few months later, Clark and I were asked to serve on a Legislative Task Force.

The purpose of the task force was to study the current laws and make recommendations for changes. Also serving on the Task Force were people who'd previously been our "enemies," including the District Attorney, John Suthers, who went on to become the Colorado State Attorney General and later, the Mayor of Colorado Springs.

We were glad that they were finally forced to listen to our side of the story, hear what we were saying, and respect our ideas.

However, a conversation I had with the DSS Case Management Director made me realize that not everyone was ready to come together, hold hands, and sing "Kum-Ba-Yah." Whenever I spoke in the group, I got an unsettling vibe from her.

One day I decided to see if my intuition was correct, and I said to her, "Your department made me feel like a bad mother because I didn't kick Clark out of the house. Do you still think I'm a bad mother?"

I wanted her to say, "No, of course not."

But she didn't. She said, "Yes."

That response disturbed me. I wanted all those who'd been involved in our case to realize that they were wrong. But she just couldn't. She was totally invested in the idea that anyone who didn't buy everything the DSS was selling was a bad parent.

Fortunately, the other members of the Task Force didn't have that attitude, and we, as a group, recommended several specific changes to the laws.

Nearly all the changes were adopted, and in some cases, became the model for other states that wanted to change their laws, also.

Dear God, thank you for helping us and for bringing Emily back home!

□◇●◇□

The Master's Hand

Of late, I've pondered pleat and fold
of fabric that is bought and sold.
Sometimes it's cut into a gown
and worn by ladies on the town.

And then again, it's sometimes stored,
collecting dust on dingy boards
in backroom shelves—a lonely place
of shabby threads and yellowed lace.

The graceful gowns that are so grand
are made so by the tailor's hand,
combined with skillful thoughts aligned
inside the Master tailor's mind.

154

But what about the tattered naps
of faded trims and fabric scraps?
What use are those supplies they keep
on backroom shelves tossed in a heap?

It's in the goods considered less,
the Master's skill is shown off best.
Transformed, their beauty is released
when Master makes a masterpiece.

-37-

Making a Federal Case Out of It

RICHARD WEXLER'S book was published in 1990. In 1991, we went to a book signing in Wichita, Kansas, where Richard personally signed our copy.

The book was appropriately titled *Wounded Innocents: The Real Victims of the War Against Child Abuse.*[13] He did a good job summarizing our whole case, including those of many others. He included quotes from interviews and reports and recounted one poignant conversation he'd had with Emily that made me cry when I read it.

> Through all this, Emily was with strangers. "They didn't tell me where they were taking me, not 'til I was there," Emily said in an interview. "They said this is your home, at least for now."

> Emily said whenever she would get upset about not being allowed to go home, the caseworker would say, "Don't blame us, it's your mother's fault for not divorcing your stepfather." They'd also say, "your mom should have kicked out your stepdad."

> Emily said the repeated interrogations scared her. "They'd ask a question, but they wouldn't let me answer it. They said, 'You were tickled here, right?' If I said no, they'd look at me like, 'Are you sure?' I was afraid, so I'd say yeah. I was afraid because I didn't

156

know what they'd do to me. They had policemen with them.[14]

Not long after Richard's book came out, a message on our answering machine startled me. It was from an assistant producer of NBC's *Today Show*, and they wanted to do a segment about our story in connection with an interview they'd planned with Richard Wexler about his book.

I called the number left in the message and arranged a time for their crew to come to Colorado Springs and film us. This would publicize the issue far beyond my wildest dreams!

By this time, Emily was living with us again, and I loved it. I was amazed at how easily she forgave me. In fact, she refused to believe that I was the one at fault, even after they kept telling her that I was the reason she couldn't come home. Only God could have sustained Emily's faith in me in the face of such relentless pressure. God also restored the relationship between Emily and Clark to the fun-loving relationship they'd had in the beginning.

The *Today Show* film crew wanted some casual footage, so they followed the three of us down the street to the park with our dog Bear. They shot video of us enjoying the park, and afterwards, they interviewed the three of us in our living room.

A few days later, we watched the two-minute segment and were pleased. They'd obscured Emily's face to protect her privacy, and they closed the segment with an interview with Richard Wexler and a plug for his book *Wounded Innocents*.

I had a few questions for God now that I was on speaking terms with Him again. Why did we have to go through this nightmare in the first place? What was the "big picture" good reason for our false accusation? How did all this fit into the verse in Romans 8:28?

> *"All things work together for good to those who love God, to those who are called according to His purpose."*[15]

The answer was eventually made clear.

M. Scott Peck begins his book *The Road Less Traveled*, with these words,

157

"Life is difficult."

No one is immune to problems, but God can create something good out of any situation.

The most important question is not *Why did this happen?*

The most important question is *What is the best way for me to respond?*

I know now that much of the emotional anguish I experienced occurred because I allowed fear to overwhelm my thoughts and emotions. Trusting God and praising Him in the storm is the best response to any adverse circumstance.

If I view our experience from a higher plane and look for the good that came from it, I will say that I watched an entire nationwide system being reformed, and I was privileged to be part of it as a direct result of our false accusation.

But why did God allow the child protection system to specifically rip our family apart?

All I can conclude is that it had to happen to enough people who were willing to stand up against it to pave the way for laws and policies to change.

Did God know in advance that Clark and I would fight relentlessly to reform the system? I wouldn't have bet on us, particularly not on me. Why did God?

After God threw a monkey wrench into my suicide attempt, I came to believe that God had tasks He wanted me to accomplish. Now I believe that pushing to reform the child protection system was one of them. God knew that, with His help, I could be one of those people who didn't give up.

The child protection system didn't know what hit them when we fought back. Along came Richard Wexler, us, and countless others who loudly shouted, "Stop! You're hurting people, you're destroying families, you're making things worse, not better!"

And it worked, although it wasn't easy and it didn't happen overnight.

Initiating change took the concerted effort of a lot of people who made great personal sacrifices. They gave up their privacy, went through the pain of constantly retelling their stories, and put up with being called the lowest of the low in the ranking of criminals—child abusers. And some, like Clark and I, were considered below even that low ranking—child molesters.

However, the journalist and author of the book that told our story, Richard Wexler, didn't have that kind of stigma.

After hearing and writing about so many heartbreaking and horrifying stories, Richard became involved in establishing a national non-profit organization called the National Coalition for Child Protection Reform (NCCPR)[16] and served as their Executive Director.

Recently, I contacted Richard and asked for more background. Here is what he said.

> *I kept finding that the facts on the ground were not matching what the most widely quoted so-called "experts" were saying. When the dichotomy between conventional wisdom and the facts on the ground became too much to bear, I wrote an article about it for* **The Progressive** *called, "Invasion of the Child Savers." That was in 1985. My wife kept encouraging me to write a book. A few years later, I listened to her and started working on* **Wounded Innocents***, which was published in 1990.*

The following year, someone who'd been involved in administration within the Child Protection System talked him into forming an organization based on what he'd learned about the system while writing the book, and that was how NCCPR came into being.

Thanks to Richard and all the others who worked so hard to make changes, on August 10, 1993, President Clinton signed the Family Preservation and Support Services Program Act.[17] It authorized nearly one billion dollars over five years to fund services to "promote family strength and stability, enhance parental functioning, and protect children."

HHS Secretary Donna Shalala stated,

> *We can no longer afford a one-size-fits-all bureaucratic method. We need an approach more tailored*

to the individual needs of each family. An approach that respects the sanctity of the family. An approach that keeps families together.[18]

Don't falsely accuse people of abuse just to keep the funding coming? Don't rip families apart based on unfounded reports? Keep families together if possible and provide services like counseling? Yes! A more positive outcome for children and families for the foreseeable future.

Dear God, thank you for always being with us and for guiding us and keeping us safe.

□◇●◇□

What You Leave Behind

It's not what you accumulate
before you go
that's important,
it's what you leave behind.

-38-

Wash, Rinse, Repeat

◻◇●◇◻

I F I STILL WORRIED excessively about what other people thought of me, I would have put my highlighted cursor over this chapter—as well as the next two chapters—and hit the delete key.

But I didn't because I can't tell this story without including the worst part.

And the best part.

So keep your seat belts buckled—I'm not done yet.

By 1993, I was ready for a change. Clark had been my partner in V.O.C.A.L. However, except for the first six weeks of our marriage, I didn't really know him as my husband—apart from V.O.C.A.L.

I was so well-known in Colorado Springs, that I couldn't shop at a grocery store without someone stopping to talk to me. Media outlets from all over the country called and asked if I would give them a viewpoint and quote from "the other side" regarding child abuse cases. It was hard on my introverted personality.

The last straw occurred when I received a form in the mail from the Colorado Springs daily newspaper requesting me to complete my own obituary in advance because I was considered "a prominent citizen."

I didn't fill it out. Instead, I got out. I'd had enough notoriety to last a lifetime, and when I asked Clark, he said he could live anywhere. His career as a pre-press expert and graphic designer meant that he could find a new job with relative ease at a printing company in any city.

Emily was in high school and living with us. She was eager for a new adventure, and I wasn't very happy with the experimental curriculum being taught in her school. Amber was living in Denver with some friends, so our move wouldn't greatly affect her.

A co-worker knew of my desire to move, and he told someone who told someone else, and the next thing I knew, I had a very good offer for a job in Dallas, Texas. It even included a relocation package, so it would end up costing us nothing to move.

In November of 1993, we moved to Allen, Texas, just north of Dallas. Clark got a job with a printing company. I checked the reputation of the public high school, and it was excellent, so I enrolled Emily in the school.

I started my new job as Director of Marketing for a company that operated Job Corps Centers for the Department of Labor. Job Corps is a program of residential centers around the country that offers free educational and vocational training to eligible young people between the ages of sixteen and twenty-four. Qualifications include a low income, no drug use or other addictions, and good behavior.

Not long after I started the job, I was shocked to learn that an aggressive local investigative TV news reporter named Becky Oliver was doing a week-long exposé series on one of the Job Corps Centers operated by the company.

My job was to work on business development and proposals at headquarters, and I'd only visited the Job Corps Center in question a couple of times, but could not imagine what she found objectionable about Job Corps. I soon found out.

Tuning into the news program that week was painful and shocking, as she reported new allegations worse than those the day before. She told of drugs supplied to students by Job Corps employees, sex orgies on the campus, and worse.

I was appalled and certain that she had to be mistaken. The following week, after hearing a popular talk radio personality, Mark Davis, talking about the scandal, I called in and told him the allegations were overblown and, in some cases, downright false. He invited me to go on his show the following day as a guest and I reluctantly agreed. I really didn't know much about the situation other than what company employees told me but felt obligated to defend the company anyway.

So much for my fresh start. History was repeating itself.

Not long after doing Mark Davis' show, I was interviewed by the FBI. Yes, *that* FBI—the Federal Bureau of Investigations—due to new allegations against our company. Only this time it was regarding our business acquisition process, which was in my purview.

Taking each employee into a room alone, the FBI asked questions about how the company obtained data on competitors and if the company shared information with competitors. Nothing they described made sense to me, and my answers reflected that.

When at home, I heard odd clicking and other noises in the background during phone calls, and with a sense of shock, I realized that our phone line was likely being tapped.

In spite of the fact that I had no hand in the operation of the now-scandalized Job Corps Center or the competitive data issues raised by the FBI, my stress level was almost as high as it had been during our false accusation in Colorado Springs.

I had reached the end of my rope and ability to cope again. My neck and back hurt all the time because I carried my stress in my muscles. I felt discouraged and beaten. Literally beaten—with a club.

My doctor referred me to a psychiatrist. He listened to my issues and prescribed an antidepressant.

Dear God, help! The water is over my head again.

◻◇●◇◻

The Thought Trap

Thoughts are getting
much too close
to memories
I miss the most.

If allowed
to wander there,
I'll sink from pain
too deep to bear.

Like a trap
disguised in grass,
the pain lies dormant
'til at last—

The thought trap tightens,
set to spring
from musings light
as a warbler's wing.

-39-

Personality Pinball

◻◇●◇◻

THE FIRST MORNING I took the newly prescribed antidepressant, I was driving to work when the drug kicked in. My head started buzzing with something that felt like electrical shock waves. I had a little trouble driving, but finally made it to work and the side effect eventually subsided.

The next day was the same, only slightly less, and the side effect continued to diminish until it was unnoticeable within a week or two.

About a month later, a vice president from our parent company paid us a visit to tell us they were closing the Dallas office, and everyone would be laid off. The vice president led me into a conference room and told me that only one person in the company was guilty of the allegations raised by the FBI, and he was being dealt with.

He also told me that, although they were closing down the Dallas location, they would like to offer me a job at the corporate headquarters in Florida because they appreciated my honesty and also my singular defense of the company during the Job Corps Center news exposé.

For my part, I wanted to end my association with the company and stay in Dallas. I soon found a new job as the manager of a proposal department in a relatively small company that manufactured and installed toll tag systems.

165

□◇●◇□

On the antidepressant, my mood and emotional stability were very much improved. It felt like the first chance I'd had in nearly 10 years to drop my shoulders and relax.

I remember telling the doctor before he sent me to the psychiatrist that I felt like I was being dragged behind a horse through a cactus patch. About a month after starting the drug, I didn't feel like that anymore. I felt quite different. In fact, I behaved quite differently. In fact, I became someone else entirely.

I was no longer an introvert. The drug manufacturers acknowledge that an increase in extroversion is a "side effect" of antidepressants, but they argue that it's a good thing because depressed people need to be more engaged with others.[19]

But the drug didn't stop there. The companies also listed "risk-taking behavior" as one of the side effects, but the doctor didn't tell me, and I didn't think to ask.

Instead of seeking comfort in the arms of my caring husband, I got bored easily and longed for adventure. Instead of enjoying a good book, I spent hours flirtatiously texting with strangers in AOL chat rooms.

My personality had been flipped on its head.

Underneath it all, I knew something wasn't right, but I overlooked it because I didn't want to think about things in depth anymore. I just wanted to have new experiences.

After a few months, I wasn't satisfied with just chatting with men online. I arranged to meet them for lunch. Eventually it progressed to movie dates and dinner. I made up excuses to Clark for my absences that weren't very plausible, but I didn't care.

I got sent home from work one day to change my clothes because my skirt was too short for the dress code. Instead of going home to change, I went shopping and bought more short skirts.

It was late 1995, and Emily was attending college in Colorado. My relationship with Clark was becoming a pale shadow in the distance.

I started going to dance halls and bars at night, allowing myself to be picked up by any guy who seemed interesting.

Eventually I realized that I'd totally lost the previous connection I had with Clark. For some reason, known only to myself at the time and unfathomable to me now, I decided that I needed to move out and get a divorce. The purpose wasn't to pursue another monogamous relationship, but rather to do anything I wanted to, moral code out the window.

Did it matter to myself that I was being a bad role model for Emily and Amber? Did I feel guilty for abandoning Clark after I'd fought so hard for his exoneration? Did I feel bad for behaving so shamefully?

The short answer is "no," not during that period. Doesn't sound much like the person you read about in the earlier chapters, does it?

No, I definitely was NOT myself.

Dear God, who am I?

-40-

Evil Twin

□◇●◇□

A YEAR LATER, I was a very different person from the person I had been my whole life. I now refer to this person as "Evil Twin." I was divorced from Clark and uncaring about who might be hurt by my behavior or whether my behavior was moral. I was reckless and only lived for the moment. I didn't go to church or pray. I didn't recognize the woman in the mirror.

I will not go into detail about all the situations that Evil Twin pulled me into, partly because I don't remember all the details. Evil Twin was not a good person. She was promiscuous and motivated by lust and a search for novel experiences and physical thrills. At that time, love did not enter into the equation and took a backseat, or, more accurately, wasn't even in the car.

I didn't love any of the guys I went out with during that time. And in fact, I had no problem dumping them when I was bored until I met one particular guy. In this narrative, I'll call him "Johnny."

Johnny had bipolar disorder[20] but I didn't realize it at first. All I saw was a charismatic, charming, attractive man six years younger than me who was exciting and fun to be with. This was his "high" side—the manic side of what psychiatrists used to call manic-depressive disorder.

I was flattered by his attention. And he captured all of my attention. Johnny was attractive—a combination of a young Billy Joel and Russell Crowe. He was a talented dancer, and when he sang "Shoulda Been a Cowboy," you would swear Toby Keith was standing in front of you. Johnny had been in a country band, but his bipolar disorder got in the way of making it in the music industry. He had the voice and stage presence but got into arguments with managers and other members of the band.

Johnny and I started spending lots of time together. I was getting hooked on the manic highs that he experienced because they fed my need for excitement and physical thrills. Within a few months, he moved in with me, and that's when I decided I was in love with him. My lust had turned to love. Or so I thought at the time.

About six months after we started living together, we got married. Three months later, I convinced him to see a psychiatrist to get medication because the bipolar disorder was starting to wear me out. When I left for work each morning, I had no idea whom I would be returning to that evening. It was like being married to ten different men. He was rarely the same from one day to the next.

But the bipolar medication changed him. He was no longer a roller coaster ride. Instead, he spent the day alphabetizing all the items in my pantry and lining them up in rows. He no longer wrote songs or sang. He started eating more—in fact, a lot more—and gained weight since he didn't want to go out dancing anymore.

We stopped having a physical relationship because he was no longer interested in sex due to side effects from the bipolar medication.

My doctor lowered my antidepressant dose at about the same time, so I also started changing—I started regaining my lost personality.

My conscience kicked in again, and most nights, I lay awake grieving for the loss of my relationship with Clark. I realized that I still loved him and missed our life together.

But I'd been gone from him for more than two years, and I was certain that Clark wouldn't take me back.

Clark was hurt by the divorce. However, he didn't treat me badly—definitely not like I should've been treated. He still talked to me. I occasionally went over to his place to borrow something, and he always seemed glad to see me. But I couldn't bring myself to believe that he would want to take a chance on me again.

One weekend, Johnny and I drove up to Cripple Creek, a small town in the foothills west of Colorado Springs, to stay at a bed and breakfast and enjoy the small-stakes gambling that was legal in the town.

Saturday evening, we were walking down the street when I was tapped on the shoulder by Wanda, Clark's sister. I was shocked to see her, although I'd known that she and Clark's mom often visited Cripple Creek on weekends. I hadn't spoken with Wanda since my divorce from Clark.

I was rattled. We'd been close, but I avoided Clark's family after the divorce. I just didn't want to think about them. But now here she was, standing in front of me. She said she wanted to talk to me for a minute, so I told Johnny to go to the casino we were headed for and I would catch up. Wanda's companions also moved further down the street.

Wanda hugged me and told me that she missed me. She said she understood about my divorce, that Clark sometimes could be difficult. Tears formed in my eyes as I thought about how much I missed her and the fun times we had enjoyed. Clark's family had always treated me like I was part of their family, always with love and affection.

I realized how much the break in my relationship with Clark had affected them. My emotions took over and I couldn't speak. I wanted to tell her that Clark had nothing to do with it. That it wasn't Clark at all, it was me. But my voice broke, and I couldn't talk.

A few weeks later, Johnny stopped taking his meds. He said they made him feel "flat" emotionally, and he didn't like it. So, the unpredictable Johnny returned. And he decided I was too boring for him. He started dating other women. While we were married. It felt like Karmic payback. He was doing to me exactly what I had done to Clark.

His dating really threw me a curve ball. When we met and I was living as Evil Twin, I didn't feel emotional pain if a guy stopped calling me or was dating other women. I didn't care.

But now I did. I was turning back into Susie and had formed an attachment to Johnny. We'd known each other for two years, and we were married for one of those years. I was distraught when he started dating one woman exclusively.

The tables had turned. I told him either he was moving out or I was. I was experiencing too much pain.

He told me that he thought I was bipolar and convinced me to see his psychiatrist. I fought the idea at first, believing that he had to be wrong. Now I realize that he was seeing the old me emerge and mistook it for signs of bipolar disorder.

Johnny was a very persuasive person in his manic state and convinced the doctor to give me medication to treat bipolar disorder. The doctor went along with it and took me off the antidepressant I was on and gave me Depakote instead.

A week later, while Johnny was out with his new girlfriend, I felt emotionally disturbed to the point of being suicidal. I looked at the drug's list of side effects, and an increase in suicidal ideation was listed. I wanted to make sure I stayed safe, so I checked myself into a hospital.

I stayed in the hospital for three days, and the staff doctors took me off the Depakote and put me back on the antidepressant I'd been on—at the lower dose.

A few days after I got out of the hospital, I called Clark and asked if I could borrow something. I don't remember what it was because it was just an excuse to see him. I went over to his apartment.

I chatted for a bit, then told him what was going on with Johnny and me. Finally, I broke down in tears and Clark just held me while I sobbed. He told me that he still loved me. That he'd never stopped loving me. That he'd always pictured us "growing old together."

It was that last comment that did it. The dam I had built to contain my feelings burst wide open, and my emotions spilled out, scraping the tender places in my heart so I could again accept the love that Clark offered me.

I went back home only long enough to tell Johnny that I was moving out and he would have to take over the apartment lease if he wanted to continue staying there. He didn't seem particularly concerned. Then I went back to Clark.

I finally saw what real love looks like. Clark demonstrated it to me that day and has continued to do so every day since.

I realized then that God had been with me the whole time. I thought I was living my life without Him, but He was making sure I wasn't raped or killed and didn't catch any sexually transmitted diseases. He took care of me through it all and—even though I didn't deserve it—He gave Clark a loving and forgiving heart.

Best of all, God still loved me, too, in spite of my dreadful behavior. God, once again, rescued me and gave me back my life.

Dear God, thank You for taking care of me, and thank You for giving Clark a forgiving heart.

□◇●◇□

My final poem "Derailing the Wheels of Injustice" is on the following pages.

The "Epilogue," which I've included to give readers the satisfaction of knowing what happened to us after 1998, follows the poem.

Derailing the Wheels of Injustice

◻◇●◇◻

Part I

Without any warning, my life was upended,
everything changed, my progress suspended.
Traveling one way, now I am not.
I was just brought
to a hold,
then a stop.
I am confused.
What should I do now?
Was I all wrong,
misdirected somehow?
Jesus, I thought
I was following You.
You were my guidance,
You were my glue.
That's what I thought
but what should I think?
Is it a ruse?
Was I hoodwinked?
Am I imagining
all this is true?
Or is it just only
my version of You?

Jesus, I'm begging You,
please if you're real,
show me the pathway
around this ordeal.
Surely You don't mean
for me to go through
this nightmare that I would hope
never comes true!

Part II

Nothing is stopping
this frightening fate!
What do they want?
My head on a plate?
The wheels keep on grinding.
I'm losing my trust.
I'm losing my faith.
I'm ground into dust.

This nightmare ordeal—
When will it end?
Or might I not ever
see "normal" again?
It's hard now to see
any path to succeed—
any way to dismiss
what the court has decreed.

One thing is clear,
and this I can say.
I now know how Jesus
felt, too, on that day,
when He also suffered
the crowd's condemnation,
when He also faced
a false accusation.

God I am slipping!
Don't let me fall
into a gulf that,
to all,
would appall.
To be honest,
I'm not
convinced You exist
or that You are really
the world's altruist.

174

Part III
Then from the bottom,
the depths of my soul,
I feel a stirring
where there was a hole.
And, from my hope,
which lay dead on the floor,
a simple small voice
says, "Open the door."

I've lost so much!
And I don't know if
I've fallen too far
off the salvation cliff.
It seems my faith
most surely has died.
But I am not dead,
even though I had tried.

So I'll take a chance
that I really have heard
the voice of a God
who heard every word
of all of the prayers
I sent up above,
and doesn't hold grudges,
He only holds love.

Slowly I rise
to my feet and endure
the rest of my fate.
Churning wheels obscure
the meaning of justice,
of fairness and truth,
concepts that I thought
were true in my youth.

Now it is clear.
People cannot achieve
or uphold all the values
we're told to believe.
Faith shouldn't rest
on what people will do.
Disappointment will follow,
mistrust will ensue.

I slowly find my way
back to the Lord.
He calls to me
and soon after, restores
my hope and my faith
in His goodness and grace.
And I walk with Jesus
each day that I face.

Epilogue

□◇●◇□

TWENTY-THREE YEARS later, God has added three beautiful grandchildren, four small dogs, and numerous other blessings to our lives.

Clark and I have had ups and downs and other curveballs over the past couple of decades, but we have stayed together—loving each other—through all of it. I no longer take antidepressants or any other psychiatric medications.

I discovered—through experiencing it first-hand—the gift of God's grace and forgiveness. I'm grateful every day that God made a way for us to have a relationship with Him through Jesus. I've been able to forgive all the people involved in our court cases—whether they know it or not—but only because of God's grace.

I also learned to see how my own mistakes and faults contributed to negative circumstances and failed relationships, such as my first marriage. Although I wrote earlier chapters from the perspective of myself at the time, God has since given me the ability to see Daryl and other people through different eyes, without the elements of blame woven into those earlier chapters.

I'm grateful that He sends His Holy Spirit to guide us. And even when we fail to be the people we want to be—even when we "color outside the lines"—God is still there. All we have to do is turn around and we'll see Him again as He reaches out His Hand and envelops us in His warmth and love. Like the good shepherd, He never stops calling out to us.

In 1995, Amber married a nice young man who spent much of his adult life in service to our country as a member of the military. His military service meant that Amber and their three children had the opportunity to live in other parts of the world, including Korea and Italy.

Amber, not surprisingly, became a writer. She still ice skates and occasionally gives lessons.

Although Emily went to college in Colorado for a time, she lived with us in Texas for about five years when she was in her twenties. After moving back in with us, she grew content with our company, going to movies and church with us, watching the TV show *What Not to Wear* with me, then going shopping with me after we were inspired to replace our not-to-be-worn clothes.

I prayed that God would send her a loving companion, someone who would be good to her, make her happy, and be a perfect fit for her introverted personality. I wasn't sure how God was going to find her a husband, though, when she never went out except with Clark and me, which limited her opportunities to meet eligible young men.

So, I thought I would help God out and create an online profile for her on Yahoo's personal ads web page. I showed it to her, of course. She didn't like the profile I created for her and replaced it with one of her own.

Not long after it was posted, she started communicating with one particular young man. Valentine's Day was coming up, and they decided to meet in person. Miraculously, he lived about five minutes from our house instead of across the country.

Clark and I wanted to meet him, too, and introduced ourselves at the beginning of her date to check him out. He understood why we wanted to do that. First check mark in the Win Column.

Emily and the young man Jake had dinner that first night. It went well. Second check mark in the Win Column. He was a personal trainer and nutritionist who encouraged Emily to eat well and exercise. Third check mark in the Win Column. They got along so well, they spent a lot of time together. A LOT of time. Fourth check mark in the Win Column? No.

I was losing her. First check mark in the Lose Column. She was too busy to watch *What Not to Wear*. She went to movies with Jake. She was too busy to shop with me. She went shopping with Jake. In fact, she spent time with Jake every day, from Valentine's Day until their marriage six months later in July 2005.

God answered my prayer! Although I was thrilled and happy that He'd sent someone so perfect for her, I wasn't sure I liked the part about losing her. I knew I was being a selfish brat, but I couldn't help feeling like that. It reminded me too much of how she'd been taken from me by the DSS.

I did get over it, though.

Emily had a beautiful church wedding. I have a lovely picture of Clark walking Emily down the aisle at her wedding, and I treasure it.

They've been married for sixteen years now and are very happy together, which makes me happy. Emily is still athletic and active, and as a personal trainer, Jake has been the right companion for her. Their idea of a perfect weekend is mountain climbing with their two dogs.

While writing this book, I got in touch with some of the people from my past. My good friend Jim was one of the first I contacted. He got married in 1991 to Micki, a nice lady I knew from my days at TRW.

I was happy to learn that he is happy. In response to my question, "What great things are going on in your life?" he sent me this email.

> *I have one granddaughter and one great-grandson. They all live in the Springs, close enough to see once in a while and far enough away to be peaceful.*
>
> *Other than that, I managed to have good jobs where I was overpaid for being under-qualified. I had to do a lot of travel, which sometimes is a good thing, but I am more of a stay-at-home guy, so several months in Hawaii, Germany, Italy, California, New Jersey, and Maryland, along with shorter trips to several other places, including Texas, just wasn't all that much fun.*
>
> *Oh, and I have been allowed to live this long without any major calamities, does that count?*

I also got in touch with Bob VanCleave to find out more about his tenure at the DSS and confirm a few details for the book.

Bob's background had been in psychology, not agency administration, so he didn't stay at the El Paso County DSS much longer. After leaving, he went into the private sector. I was happy when I learned that he was leading a Bible Study Group for a church in Colorado Springs and writing a related weekly newsletter, to which I now subscribe. We stay in touch via emails and exchanges of our respective newsletters.

I am still close with my high school friends Elli and Tina (from chapter three) although we don't get together as often as we would like because we all live in different states.

I learned many things over the years—truths that I wish I could infuse into young people so they wouldn't have to go through all the painful "hands-on lessons" I went through.

For example, I learned that God uses circumstances to answer prayers—like this one:

Dear God, please help me stop comparing myself to others.

After my transformation into Evil Twin, I had to stop. There really was no point. No matter whom I might choose to compare myself with, it was a foregone conclusion: I would come up in the loser column. Evil Twin was, well, evil. No way around it. Pride and arrogance disappeared like a mist burned off by the morning sun. No matter who you are, I guarantee you that I am worse. Without God's grace and mercy, I would be totally lost.

As I thought of all the lessons I learned, I wanted to include them in this book. I have many more stories to tell you. But then I realized that there are too many—so many, that it's a book for another day.

And I hope you will read it, too.

◻◇●◇◻

If you enjoyed *Wheels of Injustice*,
please leave a review at your online retailer and
watch for the 2022 release of my next book,
published by Soul Sonshine, LLC

To get additional content and be the first to learn of the next
book release, please sign up for my FREE newsletter. Subscribe at https://susanlouisegabriel.com

Thank you for reading!
—Susan Louise Gabriel

Endnotes

[1] ©1914 "Sister Susie's Sewing Shirts for Soldiers". *Library of Congress*

[2] Pascoe, Wolf "Going Under" from *The Sun* https://www.thesunmagazine.org/issues/421/going-under

[3] Matthew 7:7 New King James Version

[4] "Space Shuttle Challenger Explosion LIVE, January 28, 1986" KNBC live broadcast narrated by Kent Shocknek, posted by tinacart. https://youtu.be/eGLCB6CI-VY

[5] Titus, Christopher, Love is Evol "God's Will" https://www.youtube.com/watch?v=NoJGquLSUFw

[6] Luke 12:2 King James Version

[7] Matthew 10:19 New American Standard Bible

[8] Reinhold, Robert (January 24, 1990). "The Longest Trial – A Post-Mortem. Collapse of Child-Abuse Case: So Much Agony for So Little". The New York Times. Retrieved October 24, 2008.

[9] Eberle, Paul; Eberle, Shirley (1993). The Abuse of Innocence: The McMartin Preschool Trial. Prometheus Books. pp. 172–73. ISBN 978-0-87975-809-7

[10] Talbot, Margaret (January 7, 2001). "The Lives They Lived: 01-07-01: Peggy McMartin Buckey, b. 1926; The Devil in The Nursery". The New York Times. Retrieved April 5, 2008.

[11] Eberle, 1993, The Abuse of Innocence: The McMartin Preschool Trial. pp. 243–56

[12] Gabriel, Clark (1989). "About Our Cover" *VOCAL Perspective*, VOCAL Publishing Company Vol I No. 1, p. 3. ISSN 1040 8983

[13] Wexler, Richard (1990). *Wounded Innocents: The Real Victims of the War Against Child Abuse* (Prometheus Books, ISBN 0879756020

[14] Wexler, Richard (1990). Wounded Innocents: The Real Victims of the War Against Child Abuse 1990, p. 127

[15] Romans 8:28 New American Standard 1977

[16] Richard Wexler, "Bio Note," National Coalition for Child Protection Reform (NCCPR), Alexandria, Virginia, USA

[17] Office of Planning, Research and Evaluation "Family Preservation and Support Services Program Act" https://www.acf.hhs.gov/opre/research/project/family-preservation-and-family-support-services-program-fp/fs-1994-2002

[18] National Child Abuse and Neglect Training and Publications Project (2014). *The Child Abuse Prevention and Treatment Act: 40 Years of Safeguarding America's Children.* Washington, DC: U.S. Department of Health and Human Services, Children's Bureau, p. 54

[19] *Quartz*, July 12, 2016. "Antidepressants Don't Just Treat Depression, They Can Make Us More Sociable, Too" https://qz.com/727037/antidepressants-dont-just-treat-depression-they-can-make-us-more-sociable-too/

[20] Mayo Clinic, "Bipolar Disorder" https://www.mayoclinic.org/diseases-conditions/bipolar-disorder/symptoms-causes/syc-20355955

Made in the USA
Middletown, DE
08 February 2022

60827170R00118